FOUR WEEKS FOR PROSPERITY

FOUR WEEKS FOR PROSPERITY

TEACH YOUR MIND HOW TO ATTRACT MONEY USING THE LAW OF ATTRACTION WITH GUIDED MEDITATIONS, POSITIVE AFFIRMATIONS, GOAL SETTING, TAPPING, AND VISUALIZATIONS FOR PROSPERITY.

ELWYN HAYES

CONTENTS

Get more prosperity   ix

Introduction	1
Day 1 - You're prosperous and you know it	9
Day 2 - You love money!	15
Day 3 - You embrace the energy of money!	19
Day 4 - You love prosperity everywhere!	23
Day 5 - You bathe in prosperous light	27
Day 6 - Finding your abundance castle	33
Day 7 - Loving your abundance castle!	37
Day 8 - Facing your monsters	41
Day 9 - Abundance is yours	45
Day 10 - Prosperity is energy, and you carry that energy	49
Day 11 - You forgive and accept your past limitations	53
Day 12 - You enjoy the energy of money	63
Day 13 - Complaining doesn't change the weather	69
Day 14 - You focus on real goals, not crappy goals	75
Day 15 - You allow infinite intelligence to guide you	83
Day 16 - You open up for greater inspiration	91
Day 17 - You are loved and guided	97
Day 18 - You expand your idea of prosperity	103
Day 19 - You visualize your ideal goal	109
Day 20 - Success is love materialized	115
Day 21 - You love success	121

Day 22 - You carry a lucky star	127
Day 23 - You love luck!	133
Day 24 - You visualize prosperity in your next month	139
Day 25 - You allow unexpected prosperity	143
Day 26 - You take inspired action towards your true goals	147
Day 27 - Time to put it in action	153
Day 28 - You keep prosperous thoughts for life	159
Tally and recap - some of what you learned	163
FAQ	169

GUIDED MEDITATIONS

About guided meditations	175
1. Sending love to money	177
2. Sending love to money then embracing it.	181
3. Bathing in golden, prosperous light	185
4. First visit to your abundance castle	189
5. Loving your Abundance Castle	193
6. Confronting your monster	197
7. Taking the abundance castle with you	201
8. Carrying the abundance castle with you everywhere	205
9. You're guided by Infinite Intelligence	211
10. You receive your lucky star	215

TAPPING

About Tapping	221
1. Cleansing tapping for negative beliefs about money	225
2. Feeling good about money	231
3. Allowing Infinite Intelligence to guide you	235

4. Expanding your belief in prosperity	241
5. Loving and attracting success	245
6. Loving and attracting luck	249
7. Focusing on your main goal	253

VISUALIZATIONS

About Visualizations	259
1. Allow a higher power to inspire you	261
2. See your main goal achieved	263
3. Imbue your work with love to attract success	265
4. See your goal for one month from now	269

MORE EXERCISES

More exercises	273
A final word	277

GET MORE PROSPERITY

Sign up for Elwyn Hayes mailing list at
yourmind.fun
and get news and freebies.

INTRODUCTION

Congratulations!

You're on your way to more prosperity and a better relationship with money and abundance. Yay!

This book is a practical manual, with proven techniques to help you attract prosperity, and a daily program with exercises for four weeks, so that you'll know you'll keep the commitment to work on your prosperity mindset.

We'll use guided meditations, visualizations, and tapping. Don't worry if you don't know any of those. You'll learn. The idea is to train your mind to have a greater prosperity consciousness and to get rid of negative feelings towards money.

. . .

Here are some of the things you'll see:

- No more blaming yourself. Appreciate who you are.
- A super efficient technique to get rid of envy or negative feelings when you see people who are more successful or prosperous than you.
- No more crappy goals. Learn the right way to aim for what you truly deserve.
- Count on your inner guidance to reach for better goals and find prosperity.
- Learn to love success and attract success.
- Learn to love and attract luck.
- The right way to do affirmations so that they don't cause resistance.
- How to reach the right energy to present yourself better in job interviews or when closing deals.
- Make your work magnetic and attractive.
- Set long-term goals after you've done the right groundwork so that you know you're going in the right direction.

So these are some of the few things. The idea is that this book should be fun and enjoyable, while helping you achieve more prosperity in life, acting directly on your mind: conscious and subconscious!

Just the fact that you're determined to work on your prosperity for 28 days is a huge sign that you're on your way to expand it.

We all enjoy money, some of us would like to make more money than we actually do, but how much time do we devote to work intentionally on our mindset and beliefs about money and prosperity? I'd say that most people don't spend any time at all, right? And yet, if it all starts with the mind, that's where we need to work.

That's where this book comes in! The intention of this book is to help you in a 4-week ritual in which you'll work to improve and increase your prosperity consciousness.

Intentional focus can make a huge difference in our lives, and by committing to improving a certain area of our lives for twenty-eight days, or four weeks, we are training our brains to think differently, we're creating new pathways, and we're changing deep ingrained habits.

This book has practical guided meditations, affirmations, visualizations and other exercises that are sure to make quick and permanent changes in the way you think and feel. It's not enough to believe that you can attract money, you need to truly change the way you think.

Imagine a person who doesn't know how to swim and perhaps who had never seen anyone swimming before. Would belief, by itself, help this person? I'd say no. I wouldn't advise them to jump in deep water just with a strong belief that they can swim.

What about gradual exercises, starting with putting their head in the water and blowing, then floating backwards with someone beneath them, then learning to move their feet, and so on? Would that person learn how to swim? Probably. Would they need a lot of belief? I'd say no. So this is a little the idea with this book; to guide you towards a greater prosperity consciousness in a way that is gradual and natural, using powerful but pleasant exercises.

This book is not meant to be a quick confidence boost or a quick money fix. If you commit to the process, the idea is for you to make a complete change in your relationship with money, a change that will bring fruits for the rest of your life.

How much time will you need to devote to the activities in this book? At most fifteen minutes of reading and exercises daily, but also a conscious effort throughout the whole day to keep prosperous thoughts in your mind. It helps to have a little reminder every day, and that's why this book is divided into daily lessons.

I hope this book is deeply inspiring, but in small daily doses, so that you'll have inspiration for your long transformative process. Instead of forgetting it after a week or a month, my goal is for the lessons and the energy shift to ramain with you forever. I also hope you enjoy it! it's meant to be fun.

Law of Attraction, Prosperity, and This Book

This book is based on principles of Law of Attraction and other New Thought principles.

That said, I have a particular view of Law of Attraction. Thinking about attracting something means that there's a separation between you and the thing you want, let's say money in this case. I believe that instead of working on attracting things, we need to expand our consciousness and embrace the things we want. You can't attract a desire if you think the desire is bigger than you, meaning that if you believe the desire is something beyond your reach or better than what you think you deserve, you'll have trouble getting it, or you'll get it and lose it.

The work, therefore, shouldn't be just into attracting things. Sometimes you can attract things that you believe are bigger than what you can reach! Some people win the lottery, some people get a lover who they'd never guess would even look at them.

But what happens if the consciousness of the receiver isn't ready to accept these things (money, relationships) as something that belongs in their lives?

They lose them.

So attracting by itself is sometimes possible, yes, but the real work is in your belief system, so that it accommodates your desires when they show up, so that you feel they belong in your life, so that they match your vibration. This is what we're going to do with this book in relation to money and prosperity in general.

The goal of this book is not for you to understand how your mind can attract money, but rather to put this understanding into practice in fun ways and to teach your mind to expand its prosperity consciousness.

I also don't think that you need any spiritual belief or even to believe in the Law of Attraction to use this book and have a more positive attitude towards prosperity. The main idea is for you to feel good about money, believe you deserve it, and start aiming higher and reaching towards true goals. If any of the exercises strikes you as weird or if you have trouble believing in its usefulness, my advice is for you to substitute it with something else or maybe do the exercise differently. Just the fact that you're committing to enriching your consciousness for eight weeks will help you. And it's going to be fun!

How this book is organized

This book is divided into daily lessons. Many of those lessons contain guided meditations or other exercises. The end of each lesson has a summary, in case you'd like to go back and redo a day, or if you want to come back and do the exercises in the evening.

The guided meditations and other longer exercises are all included in the daily lessons and *also* included in more detail at the back of the book, so that you can find your favorite meditations and exercises easily, even after you've finished the 4-week program.

If you get the audiobook, you can play the meditations on the back of the book, lie down, and let the voice guide you. You can also follow the tappings or visualizations.

Why four weeks?

it's one moon cycle. But mostly, I think it's not too short and not too long. It's a good number of days to devote to daily exercises on a single topic. I know that some people claim that the number of days to change a habit is 21, but that is really the *minimum* number of days. The idea of twenty-eight days is to give you enough time to do visualizations, pay attention to your thoughts, change some mind habits, and really come out of this experience with a different outlook on prosperity.

Another reason for 28 days is to get into prosperous thoughts *gradually*. You could start doing affirmations now, and say: "Money comes to me easily," for example, but if you're in a difficult financial situation, that will only cause your mind to think, "yeah, right".

This would be unpleasant and make these affirmations quite useless, because they would vibrate more like "Money definitely doesn't come to me easily and I don't know why I'm trying these stupid affirmations."

Not very useful. Instead, in this book, we'll work slowly through pleasant exercises, without confronting resistance, fear, or trying to overcome beliefs too harshly. The idea is to relax and have fun with this experience.

As you're relaxing and having fun, it's easier to absorb new information and it's easier to change your thoughts.

You'll also act directly on the subconscious mind, so that it's ready for you to input more positive thoughts.

Twenty-eight days gives you the time to do it without rushing and without pressure, so that you enjoy the experience and so that it causes a permanent change in your life.

DAY 1 - YOU'RE PROSPEROUS AND YOU KNOW IT

Yay, congratulations! You're in the right path for more prosperity in your life. Let me just tell you a story. I've always believed in the power of mind and always considered myself prosperous and using well he law of attraction because all my life I had enough to live on. Wonderful, right?

Well, one day I looked at myself and said, "Well, that's stupid. If I can attract anything I want, why don't I decide to have *more* than enough?" From that day, I started trying to work on getting more prosperity, but it was pretty haphazard. I chanted some mantras I heard somewhere, I did a couple of meditations, some other exercises, etc.

Do you want to guess what happened?

Hold, hold it, drumroll please.

Suddenly my life circumstances changed and I had *less* than enough to live! Well, in truth, not really. I still had family who could lend me money, an apartment where to live, and so many things I didn't appreciate at the time.

Anyway, I blamed my law of attraction work for this dip in income. I thought that by trying to "fix" my "lack of prosperity" I was creating a mentality where I lacked prosperity, and that wasn't good. That said, a month after that, I got a good job that allowed me to live with more than enough for a long time. Until now, I hadn't connected the dots, and I hadn't realized that maybe the meditation work I'd done had actually worked, it's just that it took perhaps a bit longer than I expected.

Why am I telling you this? So that you don't despair if it takes longer than you want to see results? Yes. But at the same time, I agree with my first assessment that trying to "fix" my mentality wasn't a good idea, even if the work ended up bringing me results eventually.

So what are we going to do today? We're going to look at your own prosperity.

Today I want you to look at the things around you and appreciate them. Do you have any clothes you like? Any furniture? Is there anything nice about the house or apartment where you live? Appreciate where you are in life!

Whenever you need directions, you need two pieces of

information; where you want to go, but also where you are. Where you are is part of the way.

If you're in a really difficult situation, remember that things can change. J. K. Rowling lived for years with a modest income while planning and writing the first book in her series. Perhaps if she had a good job she wouldn't have written it, and wouldn't have become a billionaire. I don't think anyone now would claim that there was something *wrong* with J. K. Rowling before she became rich. It was just part of her process. There are many stories from rags to riches.

Okay, parenthesis here, you don't need rags, and in fact, I bet ninety percent of you reading this aren't in rags right now. This is just so that you appreciate where you are – wherever you are – in your way for more prosperity.

The fact that you want to expand is a natural desire. It doesn't mean that there's anything wrong with the way you think or with who you are. You have attracted prosperity in your life to a certain degree, and it means you can attract it. It's not something you need to learn from scratch. All you have to do is expand your already-existing prosperity consciousness.

If you happen to be in a period of great setback in life, remember the past, remember the times when you attracted prosperity. Perhaps this is your turning point. Appreciate the path that brought you here.

Today I just want you to see that you're prosperous. While you could compare yourself to people who have less, I don't think it's a good idea because you activate an energy of lack in this comparison.

Just appreciate what you have.

Running water (if you have it), a bed to sleep on, something good to eat, an outfit you like, an object you like. Look at those things and appreciate them. You can think to yourself: "it's nice to have…"

You are prosperous. You already have prosperity and the ability to attract money in you! The ability is already there. All you need to do is expand it. Appreciate what you have. Appreciate the fullness of who you are. Appreciate where you are in life, and how it has brought you here, to this moment, in the beginning of this wonderful journey.

If you've had or are having difficulties, maybe they are the ones pushing you towards expansion, pushing you towards this turning point, so there's nothing wrong with your past or your present. You're growing and expanding.

If you feel inclined, you can use the following affirmation:

> Today I recognize and appreciate my ability to attract prosperity.

I recognize and appreciate all the prosperity already present in my life.

I deeply and completely love and appreciate the fullness of who I am.

And that's it. You're already prosperous to some extent, probably to a huge extent. You came all the way here, you're alive, and you're on your way for even more expansion. Isn't that wonderful?

Summary

You're awesome. Appreciate the prosperity you already have. Appreciate nice things you have and who you are

Exercises for today: Affirmations

- Today I recognize and appreciate my ability to attract prosperity.
- I recognize and appreciate all the prosperity already present in my life.
- I deeply and completely love and appreciate the fullness of who I am.

DAY 2 - YOU LOVE MONEY!

L ove is one of the most powerful feelings you can use for visualization or attraction, and it feels good to bring up feelings of love intentionally.

Today we're going to learn how to find this feeling and you'll do an easy meditation. This meditation requires that you imagine a beautiful place, and you can think about it ahead of time, and also that you visualize a pile of cash.

Now, I know people rarely use cash nowadays, but it's still its strongest symbol. A one-hundred dollar bill is a physical representation of one hundred dollars in a way that nothing else comes close, so that's why we'll use cash.

This is Guided Meditation 1.

. . .

Sit or lie down in a quiet place. Take deep breaths to calm down your body and thoughts. Feel the air coming in slowly, slowly, then out slowly. This is very important to calm you down. Slowly, breathe slowly.

You can imagine you're in a beautiful place in nature, like a beach, forest, meadow, valley, mountain, etc. Try to feel yourself there, physically. You can smell the ocean or the leaves, you can feel the wind, the sun. Feel that you're in this beautiful, relaxing place. Now think about someone who brings you feelings of love, ideally not a romantic partner. It can be a child you love (your child or grandchild), a pet, or maybe a memory of when you were young and felt very loved.

It has to be something that makes you feel good, without conflicting feelings. If you think about a memory with your parents, focus only on the good feelings of that memory, not in whatever issues you might have. If you think about a child, try to focus on the love only.

Keep that memory in your mind and notice the warm feeling in your chest. Give it a color, preferably a warm color, like red, pink, or purple. Imagine this is your feeling of love. Love is infinite. Feeling love feels good. You can now feel that energy permeating your entire body and present in your energy field, around you. Feel yourself involved, protected, loved in that energy.

Now imagine you're standing in that beautiful place, and you see a gigantic chest, like a pirate chest, some kind of storage chest. From your heart you take a key and open it. It has so many 100-dollar bills that you know there are many millions there.

You're going to send your loving energy to that pile of cash. Just send your beautiful energy without expecting anything, without trying to feel anything, without trying to attract, just give freely.

Imbue that pile of money with your love. See it surrounded by your love. Sending love is something that feels good. Feel the pleasure of sending love to that pile of money. Say to yourself now; "I love money!"

Now you can feel yourself back where you were (your chair, your bed), feel yourself surrounded in that loving energy, feeling good.

This is a great exercise because money is said to be dirty, and in fact, bills are not clean. But beyond that, some people think that there's something wrong and "dirty" about money beyond just the germs in the bills.

By permeating money with love, you "clean" it in your mind. This is the reason it's good to do this with cash. If you find that you're having a lot of difficulty with cash, you can use bars of gold or a huge check instead. Do whatever makes you feel good. The idea is just to have positive thoughts and feelings and associate them with money.

So today your exercise is to do this meditation. It can take five minutes only, and you can even do it in bed before sleeping. If you like it, you can do it more than once a day. Ideally, though, try to take some fifteen minutes, take your time to relax, and enjoy the experience.

The affirmation for today is "I love money!", but if you do it, try to bring up the lovely and positive feelings from the visualization. Focus on bringing that good feeling to your heart, feel your heart warming, then say "I love money!"

And now you may say, "But Elwyn, I should be sending love to people, not money." Well, of course! You can send love to anyone you want, anywhere. It can help your relationships and it's going to make you feel better. Still, since money is an important part of your life, send love to it, too. After all, "you love money!"

Summary

Main idea: Money is good and it's a good idea to send loving energy to money.

Exercise: Meditation 1

DAY 3 - YOU EMBRACE THE ENERGY OF MONEY!

Today we're going to continue with the idea of loving money, at least at a symbolic level. We don't need to worry about bringing any of this to real life. The idea here is just to enjoy the exercises. Today you're going to do a guided meditation just like the one you did yesterday, with an added step.

It's meditation 2.

You'll sit down or lie down and imagine you're in a beautiful place. The same place as yesterday. You can smell the ocean or the leaves, you can feel the wind, the sun. Feel that you're in this beautiful, relaxing place.

Now bring up a lovely memory and notice the warm, loving feeling in your chest. Give it a color like red or pink. Imagine this is your feeling and energy of love. Love is infinite and the more you give, the more you have. Feeling love feels good.

You can now feel that energy permeating your entire body and present in your energy field, around you. Feel yourself involved, protected, loved in that energy. Feel the pleasure of being in that lovely energy.

Now imagine you're standing in that beautiful place, and see again the wooden chest with the huge pile of money. Send your loving energy to that pile of money. Just send your beautiful energy without expecting anything, without trying to feel anything, without trying to attract, just give freely. Imbue that pile of money with your love. See it surrounded by your love, surrounded in that loving energy in the color you chose. It should feel good, pleasant, to send your loving energy there.

Now imagine that your loving energy is transforming the money into energy. See energy the cash becoming energy. It's still money, still the same amount, just in a different form. Imagine it's a very pure, brilliant energy.

Now condense that energy in a small, brilliant ball. Since it's imbued with your loving energy, it's magnetically attracted to you. Feel that ball of money energy coming in your direction and entering your chest, then permeating your entire energetic field. Feel the pleasure of that energy in and around your body, loving money energy.

Now go back to where you are physically. Feel that the energy is with you. It makes you feel good.

Today the affirmation is "I embrace the energy of money and I allow it in my energetic field."

If you try to do the affirmation during the day, bring the warm loving feelings together with that money energy and feel it in your body. It should feel pleasant.

it's possible that some of you might feel uncomfortable bringing the money energy to your heart and energetic field, still feeling that money is not something clean. If that's the case, when you do this exercise again, spend more time sending love and feel your love purifying it.

If you're doing this without any issues, there's no need to imagine any purification, since there's nothing to purify in the first place. Do it the way it feels comfortable to you. The important thing is for you to have fun and enjoy the exercise. And this is it for today!

Summary

Main idea: to love and embrace the energy of money.

Exercise:

Meditation 2.

DAY 4 - YOU LOVE PROSPERITY EVERYWHERE!

Sometimes when we see people who have more than we do, or have things we wish we had but we don't, we're confronted with negative feelings. Sometimes it's jealousy, frustration, anger, sadness, guilt, shame, and other things. These feelings come from a sensation of separation from the abundance of the other person. An underlying thought would be, "Why do they have X and I don't?", or "Why not me?"

See, these thoughts mean that you believe you're never going to have X, and they are obviously not good thoughts. Or you could think that life's not fair, which also means you believe you'll never have X.

Another thought could be judging people as somehow "immoral" for having prosperity and a lot of money. Now, of course we might sometimes wonder about people's ethics, but this is not what I'm talking about, and this is a separate issue from the feeling of discomfort most people have when they see prosperity in other people.

This discord means that you're not in touch with your own prosperity. Now, if you keep doing the exercises in this book, you'll probably get rid of these negative feelings when seeing other people's prosperity. That said, there's a shortcut for that, and this is what we're going to do today.

Whenever prosperity catches your eye you're going to send love to it. Remember the loving feeling you learned to conjure in the meditations? It needs to be that warm feeling coming from your heart.

Try to think about a pleasant feeling, then throw a ball of loving energy at the prosperity you see. It can be a nice car, a house you like, someone's photos of an amazing vacation, anything that catches your notice.

Give it love.

This will bring up good feelings in relation to prosperity, and it's going to tell your subconscious mind that prosperity is something good.

See, if every time you see a nice car, a nice trip, nice clothes, you tell your subconscious that those things are bad and you have negative feelings, your subconscious will think that they're bad and will push them away.

Day 4 - You love prosperity everywhere!

Sending love to prosperity will put you in you harmony with it.

This is one of the most powerful techniques for prosperity, and yet it's super simple. The only thing is that you need to watch are your thoughts, or maybe it's so powerful because it's about constant vigilance against feelings of inferiority or lack.

If you keep doing this for your next 25 days, you'll already see a great shift in your life. If you turn this into a lifetime habit this will cause great, positive changes.

it's still possible that you may have negative feelings when you see prosperity you don't have, but the love you send is going to neutralize those feelings.

Also, by sending love, you'll catch those negative feelings before they make any damage.

And sending love is going to feel good! So today, whenever you see some sign of prosperity that catches your eye, send it love! Especially if you feel a bit of anger, guilt, envy, any why-not-me feeling, send it love!

The meditation for today is the same as yesterday. It will help you send love to prosperity whenever you see it. You're practicing conjuring loving feelings and harmonizing them with abundance and money. Have fun!

Summary

Main idea: it's important to appreciate prosperity wherever you see it, even if it's with other people, otherwise it means you feel separated from it or cause a separation from it.

Exercises:

- Send love to prosperity when you see it.
- Repeat meditation 2.

DAY 5 - YOU BATHE IN PROSPEROUS LIGHT

We often hear that you need money to attract money. I'm more of the opinion that your energy needs to match the energy of money and prosperity. And this is true for everything.

The great news is that you don't need to have money to have the energy of money and prosperity around you. Okay, the bad news is that you could have money and still not have the energy of prosperity, and watch that money slip away... But that's not going to happen to you, because you're here, you're determined, and you're already raising your vibration to higher levels of prosperity.

Anyway, the most important is the energy, and we're going to work on attracting the energy of money.

Today we're going to do another guided meditation, to increase even more your feeling of prosperity.

it's meditation 3. The idea is really to increase your vibration. This is a great meditation to work on deeply stored resistance in your body. It's also great because it surrounds you with positive, prosperous energy which is really helpful for any face-to-face interaction, especially concerning things like business or work.

So let's do it!

Sit or lie down in a comfortable place. Now imagine the Sun. How powerful it is, how much energy and life it sends to Earth. You receive its rays freely.

Imagine that you're receiving this gold light of the sun, and that it's literally gold and prosperity.

Imagine that it's also love from the universe, love that's given to you freely, through the gift of this powerful light.

If you believe in God or any other greater force, imagine that this light carries that energy. It's an energy of prosperity, giving, love, energy of Infinite Goodness.

See this golden light relaxing your chest. Breathe in and out this golden light. It feels good to breathe light. Then relax all your chest. Feel this loving, powerful, prosperous light in your body. Let this light go down to your stomach, relaxing your organs. Let the light relax your hips.

Feel how it's cleansing your body. It's cleansing any energy that's not vibrating in accordance with prosperity, love, abundance. It's cleansing and making all cells in your body relax in this infinite light.

See this light going to your legs, penetrating its muscles, then your feet. Feel this light massaging deeply your feet. Now feel this light coming up your legs to your back.

It relaxes and penetrates all your back. It removes tensions, removes old beliefs, old ways of thinking. You feel purified and relaxed.

Now feel this light and energy on your shoulders. They relax. Spread this light to your arms and hands. Feel how you can receive this light with your hands.

Make this light go up to your shoulders and neck. Relax your neck, then relax your throat and vocal chords. See your vocal cords vibrating with this gold, prosperous, loving light.

Now let it go to your face, relaxing all the muscles in your face, making your face brilliant with this golden light of love and prosperity.

Feel this energy coming from the tips of your hair or surrounding your scalp.

Now feel this energy penetrating your mind, your brain, taking over your thoughts. You're opening up for more prosperity, more abundance, more money.

Your mind is opening up for richer ideas. You're opening up to recognize opportunities, to attract luck and coincidences. Your mind is being programmed to attract and achieve prosperity. Your mind is being programmed with the deep knowledge that you're loved by the universe, and that you're worthy. You feel good.

Now feel this light surrounding your entire body. It's a relaxing, golden light. You feel safe, protected, secure. You can now focus on your breathing.

Breathe this light in and out. See how this golden energy is going to spread from your lungs to your entire body. When you're ready, feel your body again. Imagine that it's golden, it's shiny with golden, sparkly energy, attracting abundance.

Once you get good at this meditation, you can visualize it whenever you go, by imagining this light and breathing it. Again, this is very helpful when you want to have a more prosperous energy around you.

Today you're going to do this meditation, but don't forget to continue sending love to the things you like during the day.

Summary

Main idea: it's good to feel in line with energies of money and prosperity.

Exercises:

- Send love to prosperity when it catches your eye during the day.
- Do Meditation 3.

DAY 6 - FINDING YOUR ABUNDANCE CASTLE

Today we're going to continue working on having energetic prosperity. People who have the energy, the mindset of prosperity, attract and keep money. But it really starts with your energy. And that's what we're going to continue to work in the next days.

I want you to imagine your *abundance castle*. It can be a mansion, but it needs to be isolated, preferably in a place in nature. This *abundance castle* is going to be a place you go in your mind for your meditation, it's not a house where you'd like to live.

So you'll imagine a beautiful place in nature. It can be a beach, a lake, a forest, anything you like, and imagine this majestic building. It can be an old castle, a modern mansion, anything, really.

You're going to relax and go in this place, but before that, try to imagine some things you'll see.

Some ideas are cars, private jets, tickets to concerts, vacation tickets, prizes, furniture, chests with gold, chests with cash, chests with jewelry, your favorite perfume, cosmetics, accessories, collectibles, anything.

Your prosperity castle is a place from where you can take any riches you want, anything you want.

Once you have an idea of what this place is like, and when you have some fifteen minutes, you're going to sit comfortably or lie down for a meditation.

It's meditation 4.

Again imagine the golden light. How it's infinite, prosperous. Imagine yourself breathing this golden light and imagine it permeating, cleansing, relaxing and purifying your entire body.

Once you feel relaxed with that energy, you're going to imagine you're walking to a beautiful place and you're going to enter that castle. Touch the things there, the money, jewels, trip tickets, cars, anything. Just go to that place and enjoy the feeling. Feel the textures, smells, feel how it's solid. Walk out of it, knowing you can always come back, and feel your body again with the golden light.

That's it. Again, don't forget to keep sending love to prosperity whenever and wherever you notice it!

Summary

Main idea: We're continuing with exercises that align your subconscious mind with prosperity.

Exercises:

- Meditation 4
- Keep sending love to prosperity when you see it.

DAY 7 - LOVING YOUR ABUNDANCE CASTLE!

This is the last day of the first week. Congratulations!

We started slowly, and I would like to explain why I chose guided meditations. Well, for one, they're fun and relax you. But the most important thing is that they help you reprogram your subconscious, where years and years of suggestions and patterns are stored. It was important to start working on it, so that you'll be ready for work that engages your conscious mind and thoughts.

And then again, there's the fact that they're fun and relax you, and it means that you're not generating resistance. So keep having fun with the meditations. Don't try to make anything happen or check for any results yet, just go along for the ride, relaxing, and reprogramming your subconscious. Imagine that you're preparing the soil so that you'll be able to plant healthy plants.

Another reason why those meditations are good is because when you surround yourself with loving or positive energies, and they affect your energy field. If you have to go to a job interview, close a business, or anything that demands personal contact, you'll be a lot more likely to be successful after a meditation where you imagine loving, prosperous light around you. This is going to help you immensely!

Today we're going to do another meditation. Meditation 5. It's a combination of the two previous meditations.

When you relax, imagine the energy of the sun as this infinite abundance, and breathe it in. At the same time, remember a person or a pet you love, or a loving memory. Imagine that you're receiving love from the son, and combine this energy with your own feelings of love. You can see it as a loving energy in your chest.

Imagine it in your entire body. Now walk to your abundance castle and send love to it. Envelope it with love. Once you get there, send loving energy to everything in there. Come back, and feel a loving, prosperous energy enveloping you.

Again, don't forget to send love to everything you see that reminds you of prosperity. Do that during the day! This is very important, so that you don't have conflicting or negative thoughts about prosperity.

Summary

Main idea: We're preparing our subconscious mind so that it'll be aligned with more conscious practice about prosperity. You're also adding positive energy to your energy field, which will help you in face-to-face interactions.

Exercises:

- Guided meditation 5.
- Keep sending love to prosperity when you see it.

DAY 8 - FACING YOUR MONSTERS

It's been one week! Congratulations!

You're an awesome human being, and just your commitment to doing the work on your mind is having results. Just the fact that, for a week straight, you sat down and directed your intention and energy towards having more prosperous thoughts is extremely helpful.

How are you feeling? Have you been feeling a shift in your energy? This is great. Now, don't start wondering when you're going to see results. If you plant a seed, you know that it's coming, you don't dig to see if it's growing. With that certainty that you should continue working on your mindset.

. . .

Now, the first week was pretty easy, right? Like I said; we're going to do this gradually.

Now, many of us have fears, beliefs that we're not worthy, old programming, and other things preventing us from manifesting our true abundance. We're going to start working on these issues this week. Why didn't we start with that in the first week? Because you need good feelings to replace the bad feelings.

Last week we associated prosperity with love and positive feelings, and those exercises will make us stronger, so that we are ready to tackle our fears, insecurities, and other not-so great things . You can't simply remove negative feelings and leave a vacuum. You need something to put there, and our loving feelings about money will do the work.

During the day, keep sending love whenever you see prosperity. You're probably getting good at it. Don't forget it! it's super, super important.

Today we're going to do another guided meditation. Meditation 6. This meditation has to do with your inner child. Why child? Because that's the age when we internalize fears and beliefs, and that's the mental age of the part of yourself with those fears. Let's go.

. . .

Day 8 - Facing your monsters

Lie down or sit comfortably and relax with the golden light. Now you're going to imagine you're walking to your prosperity castle. But before the castle, there's a monster. A huge monster. It can be a dragon or something else. Imagine that this dragon carries your fears, feeling of unworthiness, negative feelings associated with prosperity, etc.

You're going to project love to this monster and walk to it without fear.

You'll touch it and hug it (you can hug its neck or leg if it's too big). As you hug it and envelop it with love, the monster will transform. It's going to become a human child, you as a child! Hug your inner child, your fearful self. It feels good to give love to your vulnerable parts, doesn't it?

Now, you're going to go to the castle with your inner child. Explore the place, have fun, enjoy the experience. Your inner child is cured. They know that it's safe to go to your castle of prosperity, they know it's good. There's nothing to fear, there's nothing wrong about going in it, there are no negative consequences. You can now hug again your inner child and you two become one. Healed. Imagine you're back in your physical place, surrounded with golden energy.

This is the meditation for today. Keep sending love whenever you see prosperity!

Summary

Main idea: We've worked on positive thoughts about prosperity and now we'll also work on tackling our fears and blocks.

Exercises:

- Send love to prosperity whenever it catches your eye.
- Do meditation 6.

DAY 9 - ABUNDANCE IS YOURS

Soon we're going to move on to new techniques and also goal setting, but it's important to keep working on your subconscious.

Today you're going to do again the meditation with your castle of prosperity, but without the monster, and with an added step. The idea is for you to feel prosperity within you.

People often say that money attracts money for example, but our world is also a world of energy. The energy of money attracts money just as much as money. This is why those guided meditations can be so helpful, since they imbue your subconscious mind with thoughts of prosperity and money. This meditation works really well because we already tackled fears, blocks, resistance, so it's really good and has powerful effects.

It's meditation 7.

Imagine the golden light of the sun relaxing your body and mixing with your loving energy. Relax your body. Now see yourself in the beautiful place in nature near your abundance castle. This time, the child is waiting for you at the entrance, and you two go together. Send love to everything in the castle. The gold, cash, objects, tickets, cars. Enjoy your experience there.

Once you get out, look at the child and imagine you say, "Want to take it home?"

The child agrees.

The castle transforms itself in golden, sparkly energy. See its walls dissolving, see it as golden, sparkly energy, see this energy consensing in a ball, now feel how you're attracting this energy to you.

Let this energy enter your chest, your heart, then permeate your body. You and the child become one again, and now you return to where you were sitting or standing.

Feel the energy around you. You have the prosperous energy of the sun, the energy of love, and the energy of the prosperity castle, and you're carrying now the castle with you!

Summary

Main idea: We're continuing working on our subconscious and increasing our feelings of prosperity. Money attracts money, so you'll have the energy of money within you!

Exercises:

- Meditation 7.
- Send love to prosperity when you see it!

DAY 10 - PROSPERITY IS ENERGY, AND YOU CARRY THAT ENERGY

You may have noticed that the meditations with the abundance castle follow a natural progression. Like I said, we're doing this gradually. Tomorrow we'll start with a new technique, but I want you to really be ready for it.

Today you're going to do another guided meditation. It's meditation 8.

You'll relax again, feeling the golden light and loving energy. You're going to walk to the place where your prosperity castle usually is, but it's not there today, which is perfectly normal. It's normal that the castle shouldn't be there. You took it with you, remember? You have the castle without you. See the energy of the castle coming out of your chest, becoming sparkly energy, then forming the walls of the castle again, the way you've always seen it. See it becoming solid.

Go in the castle and touch its walls, feel the objects. Enjoy its beauty. See how it's solid. When it's time to go home, you and the child become one again, and again you transform the castle in sparkly energy and allow it to enter your chest.

Go back to where you are, feel the energy of your castle combined with the energy of the sun, and imagine you fill the room where you are with that energy.

Imagine that this energy wants to expand, and you relax and allow it to expand. Feel it permeating the room where you are. It feels good.

Today you're going to send that sparkly, golden energy to places surrounding you. Surround your place of work with it, send it to people you love, or people that you see. Remember that it is infinite, charged with sunlight and love.

Now, whenever you pay something or if you do anything related to business, job, or money, surround the objects related to it with this sparkly energy of prosperity. This is very powerful, because it means you're giving. Give to receive. Well, you can give prosperous energy. In some cases, it might be more powerful than giving money, and it will make you feel in a prosperous position of giving.

If you need to close a business deal or do a job energy, surround yourself with that interview, also send that energy to the other person. It's very helpful because it's about giving.

Remember to continue sending love to prosperity. Whenever you see something you like, send it love. Also, remember that you're perfect where you are, and appreciate everything you've achieved, and the wonderful person you are.

Summary

Main idea: Today we're finishing the cycle of ntroductory guided meditations, and the idea is for you to carry the energy of prosperity.

Exercises:

- Meditation 8
- Send love to prosperity when it catches your eye.
- Send prosperous, golden energy to people you love, or to people with whom you do business transactions.

DAY 11 - YOU FORGIVE AND ACCEPT YOUR PAST LIMITATIONS

Today you can do any of the previous meditations when you have the time, like in the evening, but today we're also going to learn and use another technique. If you don't have time to do it today, it's fine to do it tomorrow.

Don't forget to send love to prosperity when you see it, and surround things, people, and places with sparkly, prosperous energy.

The technique is tapping, also called emotional freedom technique or EFT. The idea is to tap in certain points of your body and it helps you get rid of stored fears, anxieties, old beliefs, etc. These points are related to your meridians. If you would like to see some examples of how to do it, you can check Brad Yates or Nick Ortner on Youtube.

Caveat 1: I do tapping in a slightly different order.

Caveat 2: tapping is often used to work on negative emotions, and it's fine, as it's a cleansing process. That said, like any deep cleansing, tapping where you affirm negative emotions shouldn't be done frequently. If you find a really nice tapping session on a topic you like and it's about negative feelings, you can do it, but do it no more than once or twice, otherwise you'll be literally tapping the drum of your limitations and negative beliefs.

What we're going to do is only one session focusing on limiting beliefs, and then we'll do it with positive affirmations only.

Traditional tapping gurus might argue that the whole point of tapping is to get rid of negative feelings, and that's why it's good to recognize them, accept them, and let them go.

I'd say yes, but at the same time, any affirmation contains two sides: its meaning and its opposite. If you affirm, "I'm a millionaire", and feel discomfort because of the disconnect between what you say and what you feel, you can still tap and work on the discomfort. You don't really need to say "I don't believe that I can be a millionaire". Saying negative sentences and tapping is good in a way, to get rid of negative feelings fast, but you also have to remember that repeated words will get stored in your subconscious, so you don't want to do a lot of that.

Today we are going to do a cleansing tapping, but the negative affirmations are in the past, so it's not as problematic. If you really don't like tapping or feel it's ridiculous, you can say the affirmations while visualizing a purifying light all over you, as if you're getting rid of those feelings, but I strongly encourage tapping. Trust me, it's really powerful.

You can tap on only one side of your body, using your dominant hand, tapping with your three fingers; index, middle and ring. You tap several times softly. The points of tapping are:

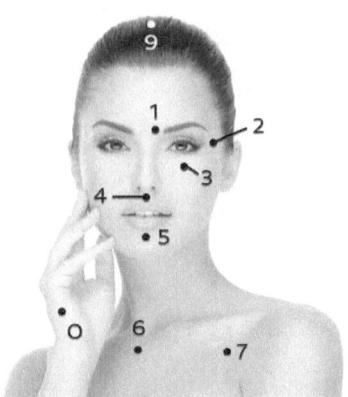

0 - Karate chop. This is the side of your hand between the wrist and your little finger.

1 - Third eye. It's not really your third eye, but the inner part of your eyebrow, near the top of your nose. If you're wearing glasses, you can do it between the eyes.

2 - Temples - outer side of the eye, near where your eyebrow ends.

3 - Under the eye - above the top of your cheekbone, at the limit where you would put concealer to hide dark circles. Be gentle there.

4 - Under the nose - between your nose and upper lip

5 - Chin - between chin and lower lip.

6 - Collarbone - Right where you would have a tie knot

7 - Scapula - Attention because a lot of tapping teachers don't use this point, and it's the one where you can feel the change immediately. It's in the middle of your shoulder blade. If you move your shoulders forward, it's the part that is most depressed in your shoulder blade. It's between your collarbone and of your shoulder. Don't worry about being precise, but don't forget this point.

8 - Under your arms. If you wear a bra, it's right over your bra, under your arm. In this place you should tap with the palm of your hands.

9. Top of your head. Here you can use all of your five fingers.

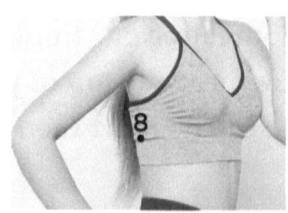

The idea is to start with the Karate chop, and then move through the other points, from one to nine, while doing the affirmations.

Here's the exercise for today (or tomorrow, if you don't find the time today, or if you want to take the time to learn a little more about tapping before doing it).

Tap on your karate chop point. Repeat: As I am getting ready to expand and allow more and more prosperity in my life, I choose to let go of old beliefs and habits. Even though I sometimes felt afraid of having money, I forgive and I accept myself deeply and completely.

Even though sometimes I felt that I wasn't worthy of having more money, I deeply and completely forgive and accept myself and everyone else who might have contributed to those feelings.

Even though sometimes I felt that life was unfair to me, or that somehow I had bad luck or wasn't destined for prosperity, I choose to love and accept myself, and, most of all, forgive myself, for these and any other limiting beliefs I held in the past.

Even though sometimes I decided to aim low, for fear of disappointment, I choose to deeply and completely love, forgive, and accept myself. I deeply and completely accept myself despite any limiting or misguided beliefs or feelings I have held in the past. A love and appreciate the fullness of who I am.

I'm now healing and moving on.

Tap on your third eye. Sometimes in the past, I might have felt that I didn't deserve money, or that I shouldn't ask for more money.

Tap on the side of your eye. I felt that I wasn't good enough, or that life came with a limit, a limit I shouldn't dare pass.

Tap under your eye. Maybe I was afraid, maybe I thought that having more money was wrong, maybe I decided to settle for less so as not to be disappointed.

Tap under the nose: Maybe I just didn't know better.

Tap on your chin. Some of these feelings might have caused me to feel bad. I even might have felt jealous, angry, upset, disappointed, ashamed.

Tap on your collarbone. These feelings were not fun and were not nice, and the reason they made me feel bad was because they were not in alignment with my true self.

Tap on your scapula. My true self is prosperous and believes in infinite source and abundance. My true self knows that it deserves anything it wants, and I'm ready to embrace my true feelings of prosperity.

Tap under your arm. I'm releasing any and every negative feeling and limiting beliefs about money from my body, my mind, and my energetic field. They're gone.

Tap on the top of your head. I release any feelings of envy or discomfort about other people when they have prosperity. I understand that there's enough prosperity to go around, and I understand that I can have as much as other people, and each of us is unique.

Tap on your third eye. I release any feelings that I should ask for little, that I should limit myself to little, that I should feel content with little. There's no need for me to limit myself. I allow myself to reach for the stars. If anything, it feels much, much better!

Tap on the side of your eye. I release any feeling that I'm not worthy. I'm a wonderful, unique, magnificent child of the universe, and I deserve good things. My worth is infinite. I am worthy.

Tap under your eye. I let go of the need to limit myself. While there's beauty in struggle, there's also beauty in achievement, there's beauty in reaching for more, achieving my dreams, helping people.

Tap under your nose. I let go of any fear that money might be dangerous for me or for the people around me. I feel the good that I can do with money, and I decide to allow more and more money in my life.

Tap on your chin. I choose to align myself with prosperity, and to allow prosperity and money in my life, mind, body, and energetic field.

Tap on your collarbone. I feel the energy of money and abundance entering my life, and I allow more and more of it.

Tap on your scapula. I choose to release from my body, my mind, my spirit, and my energetic field any fear, any limiting belief, any negative thought that has kept money away from me in the past. It feels good and natural to let go of these old beliefs because my real nature is prosperous.

Tap under your arm. I feel great now that I have eliminated any feelings that don't serve my prosperous nature. I feel great now that I'm open to my true prosperity, now that I recognize my real worth.

Tap on the top of your head. I choose to allow more and more money in my life, and I know it's safe, it's good, and it's in line with my inner self.

Tap on your third eye. I can do good with money, I deserve as much money as I want, and I choose to align myself with abundance and prosperity.

Tap beside your eye. I vibrate in alignment with prosperity. I attract money and opportunities, and I manifest my true self and my ideal life. I feel great about it.

Tap under your eye. I love money and money loves me. I

love to see prosperity in my life and in other people's lives.

Tap on your chin. I understand that I'm worthy of money, and this understanding fills me with happiness and warmth.

Tap on your collarbone. I feel thankful for all the money that I have and all the money that's on my way. I know I deserve it, and I'm excited to use it.

Tap on your scapula. Money brings me joy, and this joyous feeling attracts more and more money in my life. I'm excited, thankful, and happy.

Tap under your arm. It feels great to allow money, and I feel great right now.

Tap on the top of your head. It feels great to let abundance and prosperity permeate my thoughts, my body, and my energetic field. I embrace it in my life.

Now take a deep breath. Notice how you feel.

You should feel lighter and better, and if you had yucky feelings about money, they should be much lighter now.

We'll do more tapping in the next few days. You can repeat this tapping session when you feel you need to clean up, but then move on to more positive tapping sessions.

As always, when you see prosperity, send it love.

You don't need to be searching for things to send love to anymore, but whenever something catches your attention, let's say someone has the job you'd like to have, send love to that person and that job.

You can do any of the guided meditations at night, if you want.

Summary

Main idea: it's good to work directly on your limitations and blocks, and tapping is excelent for that. That said, don't do tapping that repeats negative feelings too often.

Exercises:

- Learn about tapping
- Do tapping 1 (or leave it for tomorrow if you want to take the time to learn the technique better).
- Send love to prosperity when you see it.
- Send prosperous energy to at least one person.
- If you have the time, do one of the previous meditations. I recommend meditations 2, 3, 5, 7, and 8.

DAY 12 - YOU ENJOY THE ENERGY OF MONEY

We're still working on getting positive feelings about prosperity. This work is so, so important!

Before doing affirmations, before setting goals, it's important to do some housecleaning to get rid of limiting beliefs and to plant the seeds of prosperity, or at least get your creative soil ready for prosperity. These exercises should help you shift your energy, too.

Today we're going to do one more session of tapping. If you like this session, you can repeat it as much as you want because it focuses only on positive feelings associated with prosperity.

You might notice that this session focuses a lot on feelings, saying that you feel good, you feel happy, etc. That's because emotion is a must whenever you do meditations, affirmations, or visualizations. Tapping is about getting rid of negative emotions, and for that, we'll focus on the positive emotions that should replace them.

Other than the tapping session, you can do a guided meditation if you want. Keep sending love to prosperity when it catches your notice. And send sparkly, prosperous energy to at least one person, place, or object you see.

The tapping session for today is this (tapping 2):

Take a deep breath, and think about your relationship with money. Just think about money. Bring it up in your mind. When the image is clear, start.

Tap on your karate chop: I'm ready to open up for more prosperity, abundance, money. I allow prosperity in my life, and allow more and more prosperous thoughts. I choose to believe that money is good, that I deserve it, and that I am worthy of everything I want. I choose to aim for prosperity and abundance, with the deep knowledge that I deserve it. I release any feelings of fear, unworthiness or doubt while at the same time forgiving and loving myself deeply and completely and appreciating the fullnes of who I am.

Tap on your third eye: I allow abundance in my life. I release any fear, limitation, or misguided thoughts that could interfere with this abundance.

Tap on the side of your eye: I choose to feel good about money, and feel confident in my ability to attract money and to keep money.

Tap under your eye: I feel prosperity increasing in my life. I allow it to increase, I feel it increasing, and I feel great about it.

Tap under your nose: More and more prosperous thoughts come to me. I feel aligned with prosperity, aligned with money, and attracting money.

Tap on your chin: It feels good to allow money to come to me. It feels good to increase my prosperity.

Tap on your collarbone: It feels natural to let money come to me, and to attract opportunities.

Tap on your scapula: Feeling good about money feels right, feels natural.

Tap under your arm: More and more I see my prosperity increasing, and I feel good about it.

Tap on the top of your head: it's natural to have extra money in my bank account, and I love having extra money there.

Tap on your third eye: it's great to always have extra money, and to have more and more extra money every month.

Tap on the side of your eye: I feel that I'm expanding my ability to attract money, and money is coming to me more easily.

Tap under your eye: More and more I'm getting better paid for what I do or what I sell. I get better clients, better opportunities, bringing me more and more money.

Tap under your nose: I allow good opportunities to come to me because I know I'm worthy and deserving of them.

Tap on your chin: I'm confident in my ability to attract money and to be valued and appreciated for the wonderful being that I am.

Tap on your collarbone: I feel that I'm worthy, deserving, valuable, and it's natural that the universe recognizes that and brings me prosperity.

Tap on your scapula: I am confident and happy about having more and more money in my life. I deserve it and I can do a lot of good with money. I enjoy feeling the energy of prosperity in my body, mind, and energetic field.

Tap under your arm: I'm excited about having more money. It fills me with joy and happy anticipation. I enjoy vibrating in harmony with prosperity.

Tap on the top of your head: I expect good things to happen, I expect money to come to me.

Tap on your third eye: it's natural for me to attract great, well paid opportunities.

Tap on the side of your eye: I see my bank account with more and more extra money every month, and it's natural.

Tap under your eye: I see better and better, greatly well paid opportunities coming my way. I know they are right for me and I deserve them.

Tap under your nose: It feels right to earn a lot of money, it feels natural. I feel great and confident about it.

Tap on your chin: I enjoy having a lot of money, and I enjoy spending it and spreading prosperity around me.

Tap on your collarbone: it's right for me to earn a lot of money.

Tap on your scapula: It feels natural to see my bank account with more and more extra money every month.

Tap under your arm: It feels good to know deeply that I'm worthy and deserving of great prosperity.

Tap on the top of your head. I'm happy to be aligned with the energy of money. I allow this energy in my body, mind, and energetic field.

Summary

Main idea: We're tapping on positive feelings to get rid of negative feelings and eliminate blocks and limiting beliefs.

Exercises:

- Send love to prosperity when you see it
- Send abundant, sparkly energy to at least one person or one place
- Do tapping 2
- If you have time, repeat a guided meditation. 3 and 8 are especially recommended.

DAY 13 - COMPLAINING DOESN'T CHANGE THE WEATHER

Today the exercise is to repeat the tapping from yesterday. It should really clear any blocks you still have about prosperity. Other than that, like always, send love to prosperity when you see it, and remember to surround yourself with prosperous, sparkly golden energy. If you have the time, repeat one of the guided meditations.

Today I want to talk about something else, though: complaining. Complaining about how things don't work, how things are difficult, how things are unfair, only increases that energy in your life, and this is a habit you must stop. Now, there are two kinds of complaining; *whining* and *asking for a correction*. Asking for a correction is good. Whining only maintains the status quo.

I'll give you an example. You go to a restaurant, and they

send you the wrong dish. shouldn't you complain? For sure, but that's the "asking for a correction" type. You call the waiter and explain the issue. It's very likely that they'll bring you the right dish. It's good and it works. You'll be happy and might even return there one day.

Now, whining would be "oh, look what they brought me. These people are incompetent, etc." Whining doesn't fix the problem, instead, it accepts the problem as a natural occurrence. It also increases negative feelings in you, and you might eat something you don't like. It doesn't help!

So stepping up against injustice, mistakes, doesn't really count as complaining, even if t's sometimes called camplaining. Asking for corrections is good.

The problem is in whining. Even mental whining is bad. "This sucks", "it's always hard," "The good ones are taken," etc. Don't indulge in those thoughts. They don't help you.

I once noticed that complaining is not good and I set the intention of spending one month without complaining. Now I'm better at it, and as long as I'm aware, I can go without complaining for months in a row. But when I started, I had to pay attention, but I did well throughout the day.

The problem is that I live in a very cold place, with very dark winters. So imagine when I woke up at six, while it was still dark, looked at the weather app and learned it was -20C (-4F). I looked outside and thought "it's so cold! it's so dark!" Well, that's whining complaining. Yes, it's cold. Yes, it's dark. But guess what? Complaining doesn't change the weather. I could use my mental energy to think about something better. You can use your energy to think about something better.

Now, there's another type of complaining, which is not really complaining; venting or opening up. Telling someone about your problems is not complaining, unless you're going about it on and on. Telling someone about your problems, and talking about difficulties can help you face them and find a solution. It's good. It's more like "asking for a correction". It's different.

Complaining as in *whining-complaining* is a kind of energy people indulge in. I see it online, in groups, I see it at work. Try to avoid these behaviours. Whenever people are going on and on about how things are hard, difficult, unfair, try to talk about something different.

You don't have to avoid people, just don't indulge in complaining. I participate in writers' groups online. You bet there's a crowd complaining against Amazon, complaining that it was easier before, complaining that you need money for ads, etc. Meanwhile, there are people sharing victories, sharing tips, sharing success stories. With which group can I learn? The second group!

If someone posts a warning about a negative experience,

that's one thing; that's learning, but circular whining about difficulties is really counterproductive.

Avoid it in your personal life, and most of all, avoid it in your professional life. Choose to give attention to people who achieve things, not to people who complain that they can't achieve.

Choose to interact in situations where you seek solutions, not complain about problems. And sure, you can mention problems if the goal is to solve them, but not mention problems as a status quo that you're upset about. It doesn't help

Complaining doesn't change the weather. That said, you can get a better coat, maybe get a lamp with blue light to compensate for darkness, maybe an alarm clock with gradual light. There are tons of things you can do. If you want to talk about the cold and the darkness, seek solutions, don't just complain about how bad they are. When you whine-complain, you just assume that there's nothing to be done about it, and it can really set you back.

So today I want you to pay attention to your interactions, and avoid those where there's whine-complaining. If you have colleagues or friends who like that, try to change the subject. You might even help them! And watch your mind, too. Whining complaints in thoughts are just as bad as spoken whining complaints. So avoid them.

As an exercise, repeat the taping from yesterday. It's really powerful and can shift your energy towards prosperity. Keep giving love to prosperity when you see it!

Summary

Main idea: Avoid complaining, whining complaining, and avoid interactions just to complain about how things are bad. They don't help you.

Exercises:

- Repeat tapping 2.
- Be aware and avoid complaining for the sake of complaining.
- Send love to prosperity when you see it.
- Send golden, sparkly prosperity light to at least one person or place.

DAY 14 - YOU FOCUS ON REAL GOALS, NOT CRAPPY GOALS

If you're used to Law of Attraction methods, and even psychological methods for prosperity, motivational coaching, etc. you might be wondering when we're going to start with goal setting and precise visualizations.

This is one of the first things you usually do, right? Abraham Hicks, which is still one of my favorite Law of Attraction coaches, says you have to ask, believe, and receive. Fine, to be fair, a lot of the Abraham discourse has evolved and this is an unfair oversimplification. Still, when thinking about prosperity, we usually consider that it's important to have precise goals, or ask.

Well, I agree! However, and there's a big however here, first we need to be ready to ask. You should be much better by now, with all the exercises we've been doing.

Second, we need to think: what kind of goals? Sometimes our mind is a mushy mess of things we think we should want, we think would make our lives better, and even things we think we want, but don't really.

People often set goals that aren't great for them. People sometimes even use law of attraction to achieve these goals. And law of attraction works, whether you use it consciously or not. You can attract the crappy job, start the business you hate, even spend years studying something you realize is not for you.

Sometimes we really want A, and we believe that in order to bet A, we need to get B first. Then we set our intention, energy, goal setting on…B! Which wasn't even what we wanted.

I'll give you an example of my life. What I really want is to make money from my writing. I'm mostly a fiction writer. I know that it's possible, and that it's a matter of working hard, writing consistently, and writing books people love. I'm well on my way now, and my prosperity has been increasing incredibly fast while I'm doing what I love. That said, it took time. I know it and I had to eat meanwhile, so I needed a job.

I applied and applied for full-time jobs, but couldn't get one. But hey, most of these jobs would make me extremely unhappy and wouldn't give me time to write. So I didn't want them. But I wanted them—to have money.

Day 14 - You focus on real goals, not crappy goals

You can see how well that went, right? Didn't go well, but see, the fact that I didn't get these jobs didn't mean there was something wrong with the way I was thinking or that I wasn't using Law of Attraction. I was. I didn't want those jobs, and didn't get them. Great. Now tell that to stupid, conscious me, who spent a lot of time every day sending resumes and polishing cover letters.

I am also an ESL teacher, which is great because it's often part time. For some stupid reason I still don't understand, I set the goal of working at a specific school. It was a long time ago, I saw the job ads, and said, "I'll work there." It wasn't goal setting as in focusing, visualizing, but more like a spur of the moment thing, seeing it, and deciding I'd work there.

It was a prestigious school and I thought it would prove something about my teaching skills, help me improve as a teacher, or I don't even know.

You want to guess what happened? I worked there!!! No kidding, genius.

Want to guess what else happened? I hated it.

I hated the methodology, and the fact that it was part time even in the summer, when ESL teachers are getting full-time temporary work where I live, which would have been better for me. I didn't do it consciously, setting the goal to work there, but somehow I did.

And now you may ask, "So Elwyn, is your greatest goal in

life to become an ESL teacher at a language school?"

Let me shake my arms in despair, "NOOOOOOO!"

Why the bleep did I set those goals? I think I was under the impression that a part-time teaching job would be good for me. That is true, but I shouldn't pick the school where I want to work. In fact, considering my real goal isn't teaching, even though I think teaching is super fun, I shouldn't even be setting goals for teaching. Recently I started doing translation and other types of work which pay more, take less time, and don't require commuting. They were much more helpful in sustaining my goal.

I made another huge mistake. Like I wrote earlier, my goal is to be a fiction writer. I thought I had to study, and I went on to study Creative Writing in university. It was a lot of fun, I learned a lot, but it didn't help me much.

I only really started dipping my toes on the possibility of being a successful fiction writer when I learned about indie publishing and got involved with writer groups. I had never done any of that when I was studying. I guess I thought that being with my classmates, under the impression of being in a writing scene, made me feel I was going in the right direction. I wasn't, but I was so caught up with the university that I didn't notice it. Yikes.

it's fine. I learned. That said, I could have saved years of struggle if only I had been open to other and better alternatives, if only I had been focused on what I really

Day 14 - You focus on real goals, not crappy goals

wanted, and had started taking the right steps towards it. I could have still studied, but I should have known that my goal was not contained in the school and I should have searched for where to find it.

it's not only me. I know a lot of people who decide to take a profession and realize they have to study to achieve it. Great! Studying is amazing for so many reasons other than just being able to work on a specific profession. Studying is great. That said, again, sometimes it's a program that's difficult to get in. So people focus on getting in. Sometimes it's hard to get good grades, get a certain prize, scholarship, whatever, while in the program, so people focus on these things. Sure, it's good to focus on the process.

That said, again, sometimes people get so involved in the short-term goals that they forget their long term goals. Sometimes excellent students graduate and can't find jobs in their area. Why? Could it be because they spent so much focus and energy on the results of their studies that they forgot the real goals?

So my advice for you is not to do that. Always keep the end goal in mind, always remember why you are doing something, and where you want to go in life.

Life distracts you.

Sometimes we go to the grocery store to buy A, and come out with X, C, Y, F, but not A. Yep. It happens.

Focus.

Don't get caught up with crappy goals. Sure, sometimes your bigger goal has steps to achieve it. You can focus on the steps, like passing an entrance exam, but make sure you never, ever lose sight of where you really want to go.

And be open. Sometimes you focus on a certain strategy to achieve your goal that's completely wrong, and maybe you would have noticed it if you kept the end goal in mind, and not the middle steps.

Hey, there's nothing wrong with those experiences. First of all, they are all experiences, second, sometimes you need to know what you don't want in order to find clarity about what you do want. Of course, you want to do better now, but rejoice the opportunity you've had for learning.

Also, if you've ever attracted a crappy goal, you should pat yourself on the back and rejoice! It means your attraction is working, and you should feel proud that you reached your goal, whatever it is.

Sometimes it's also a matter of expansion. What you may now think as a crappy goal was a huge deal back then, and it was a step towards bringing you where you are right now, so it's good.

That said, let's try to attract better goals, goals that will bring prosperity more easily, goals that will take us quicker to where we really want to go.

And now you may ask, "But why does law of attraction allow us to attract the crappy job?" Well, free will, for one, and second, you can think of it as energy. Gravity is not evil when you fall, and good when it keeps your dinner on your plate. It's there, and you use it as you want.

And how can you get better goals? Well, you can choose to have better goals and let Law of Attraction help you. You can also choose to keep your real goals in mind, and beware of crappy goals. They're everywhere.

We should absolutely set goals, but they should be based on what we really want. Even our final, big, real goal, can be muddled and hidden under a cloud of false beliefs. So what do we do? We set the intention of being open to a higher intelligence, higher power, and to listen to what it tells you.

We waited this long to start focusing on goal setting for prosperity because it was important to align with prosperity and to get rid of negative feelings and limitations, otherwise you could be setting goals from a position of lack; our infamous crappy goals. This is why this book is a slow process. Now we're about to get ready to establish goals.

The exercise today is a goal intention before sleeping. Ask and decide to receive guidance on how to achieve prosperity, how to achieve clarity in your goals. Even if you're super clear about what you want, this can help you fine tune your desire.

We'll work on setting a goal for two years from now, but depending on what it is, it could be a shorter period or longer. Sleep on it. What do you really want? Where do you want your life to go? This is the exercise for today. Other than that, as always, keep sending love to prosperity when you see it!

Summary

Main idea: want and focus your energy on what you really want, not what you think you need to get what you want. It's important to be aligned with prosperity before setting your goals, so you don't settle for crappy goals.

Exercises:

- Before sleeping, set the intention to receive guidance about a prosperity goal for about two years from now (or later or earlier depending on the goal). Don't set the goal yet, just the intention to receive clarity about it.
- Repeat tapping 2 and guided meditation 8. Pick only one if you don't have the time for both.
- Send love to prosperity when you see it.
- Send golden, sparkly, loving energy to a person or place.
- Avoid complaining.

DAY 15 - YOU ALLOW INFINITE INTELLIGENCE TO GUIDE YOU

All right. It's been two weeks! Yay, you awesome human being! And now we're getting ready to set goals.

Real goals.

If you've been following the book daily, just the habit to spend some fifteen minutes a day to increase your prosperity consciousness has been super helpful. What a great journey, and what a great habit.

Rejoice, pat yourself on the back, and do a little dance if you want to.

So yesterday I told you about the infamous *crappy goals*.

And you started thinking about your real goal. For that, you can ask to receive higher guidance.

Why ask for and use a higher guidance? Because it's logical, even if people tend to skip this step.

Moving without direction is not very efficient. It's like a person who goes to a new town, trying to find an address, but doesn't use GPS or doesn't even ask. Yeah, you might know someone like that. It's illogical, right? But it's based on the false premise that you know how to get there. By the time you find out you don't really know, you've wasted some time of your life.

In the case of a visit, it can be a few minutes. In your life... Well, everything is valid as a learning experience, but you can be a bit more efficient, right? So focus on guidance, even if it's your own, inner guidance. Get that GPS to work and trust it.

Today, we're going to work more on connecting to a higher intelligence. It can help you set better goals and help you see your objectives more clearly, but it can also help you feel more inspired and take better professional decisions, for example.

This is a key point in prosperity that most people skip; asking for inspiration, asking for guidance. Isn't prosperity often about having good ideas? Well, why would anyone skip that? Let's tap into a higher intelligence, then.

Where does that intelligence come from? You can imagine it comes from your subconscious mind, now attuned to the vibrations of prosperity. You can imagine you tap into collective consciousness. You can believe it's the intelligence of the Universe, or God. As the sole power in the world, it permeates everything, and if we want, we can reach out and allow it to guide us. This is my personal favorite, but it doesn't matter what you call it or where you think it comes from, as long as you feel and know you're connecting to something greater than just your conscious mind.

We'll call this source of knowledge and inspiration *higher intelligence* and *infinite intelligence*, *higher inspiration* and *infinite inspiration*. Connecting to it can make a huge difference in all steps in your life, and it might be one of the most powerful techniques for prosperity.

Again, higher intelligence can help you with inspired action and can also help you even your goals more clearly and set better goals. Opening up for guidance is one of the most powerful techniques for prosperity, because it guides the way to get there.

Today we're going to do a visualization. Visualization 1.

Visualization is different from the guided meditation because in a visualization you're awake, aware, and sitting down. It's important to sit down with your spine straight and with your palms facing up. There's a reason for that, so get in this position and you'll see how the visualization flows better.

Take slow, deep breaths, breathe in and out. Imagine a silver and purple light coming from above and entering your mind and your energetic field. Imagine that this is a light containing higher intelligence; intelligence from the universe, your subconscious, the collective conscious, a superior power or God, your higher self, or all of it. See this light reaching you and how you're allowing it.

Say or think these words:

> Today I choose to allow infinite intelligence to guide me.
>
> I open up and allow it.
>
> I open up to infinite guidance so that I can set my true goals with clarity.
>
> I allow infinite intelligence to help me set more prosperous goals, in line with my true self.

Imagine now this light of infinite energy. Imagine you're receiving it. Feel happy and thankful for receiving this guidance. Feel inspired. Feel trust in your higher guidance. Feel safe.

Take deep breaths and go back to where you are. See this energy around you. Feel that this light is going to guide you from now on, and be open to sudden bursts of inspiration or intuition.

Try to feel throughout your day that you're being inspired by a higher intelligence.

Now, as much as you should act on inspired action, it doesn't mean you should take rushed decisions.

Trusting infinite intelligence also means giving it time to give you answers. So if you have to make a decision concerning an investment, or if you think you want to buy something that costs a lot, wait. Before committing to it, wait at least one day, and, before sleeping, ask for guidance whether it is a good thing or not.

Some scammers and some genuine sellers have offers that compel you to take action right away. Why do they do that? Because they know that if you wait, if you think about it, you'll realize that what they are offering is not that great. Whenever you see any "act now" offer, be aware, and instead of buying it, wait. Listen to your inner guidance. Don't rush into decisions, don't rush into large expenses. Use the guidance available to you, and you'll make smarter decisions.

Other than that, today keep sending love when you see prosperity. Also, before going to bed, set the intention to receive guidance about your true goal for two years from now, this time feeling that you're connecting with a higher intelligence. You can also repeat a tapping or meditation if you have the time.

Summary

Main idea: connecting to a higher guidance will help you establish better and clearer goals and it will also help you take better business and professional decisions. That said, just because you feel that you have higher guidance and trust your intuition, it doesn't mean you should rush into decisions. Give your inner guidance time to act and help you.

Exercises:

- Visualization 1
- Before sleeping, set the intention to receive guidance for a prosperity goal for about two years from now, a goal you really want and is good for you.
- Send love to prosperity when you see it.
- Repeat tapping 2, a guided meditation, or do both.

- Complaining for the sake of complaining should no longer be your jam, so avoid complaining situations.

DAY 16 - YOU OPEN UP FOR GREATER INSPIRATION

We're going to continue working on allowing infinite intelligence and guidance so that we'll be ready for goal setting in a couple days and so that we can attract prosperity more easily, since inspiration and good decisions can help it so much.

Opening up for inspiration and for infinite intelligence can help you with better ideas, help you with smarter choices, and help you with inspired action. This is why this step is so, so important. Prosperity can often depend on luck or on smart ideas, and opening up for a higher intelligence will help you with both, since intuition will help you be at the right place at the right time.

Today we'll do tapping to work on allowing guidance from Infinite Intelligence. Tapping 3. Other than the tapping, as always, continue sending love to prosperity when you see it and surround yourself with prosperous energy at least once a day.

You'll also set the intention to have a prosperity goal, a real prosperity goal for about two years from now.

So let's go to today's tapping session. The idea is for you to change old patterns and beliefs. Letting higher intelligence guide you means letting go of old habits, and it can be scary because it can feel like losing control. That's why tapping is important. Tapping works on your fears, old patterns, and old beliefs.

Let's go:

Take a deep breath, and imagine yourself being guided and protected.

Tap on your karate chop: Today I recognize that there's an infinite intelligence that knows more than I do. I choose to trust this higher power and infinite intelligence. I choose to allow it to guide and inspire me. I deeply and completely appreciate the fullness of who I am and I choose to relax and allow infinite intelligence to guide me.

Tap on your third eye: I open up for infinite intelligence. I feel myself relaxing and opening up for this powerful energy.

Day 16 - You open up for greater inspiration

Tap on the side of your eye: I choose to relax and surrender, and realize that I can count on higher inspiration.

Tap under your eye: It feels good not to need to control or decide everything, and instead to feel deeply inspired.

Tap under your nose: I relax. Surrender. Trust the universe to guide me, to give me better ideas, to point me in prosperous directions.

Tap on your chin: I release any fear or resistance to trusting the higher intelligence.

Tap on your collarbone: I attune my intuition to prosperity, and allow it to guide me into a more abundant, fulfilled life.

Tap on your scapula: I know that I'm still in control of my fate, I'm just having help to achieve what I really want, I'm accepting powerful help to fulfill my plein potential.

Tap under your arm: I surrender to a higher intelligence, a higher power, and I open up to its guidance and inspiration.

Tap on the top of your head: I choose to act in alignment with prosperity, and to trust the universe to guide me into this alignment.

Tap on your third eye: It feels good to be attuned to my intuition, it feels good to open up to infinite intelligence and infinite wisdom.

Tap on the side of your eye: I release any need to block or judge this guidance from infinite intelligence, and I allow it to direct me to prosperity and fulfillment.

Tap under your eye: More and more I recognize signs of infinite intelligence guiding me, and it feels great.

Tap under your nose: I feel sudden bursts of inspiration. Amazing ideas come to my mind. I allow these ideas to flow and materialize.

Tap on your chin: My goals become clearer, better, in line with my inner self, in line with prosperity.

Tap on your collarbone: My ideas are sharper, smarter, they lead me to prosperity and fulfillment faster and more easily.

Tap on your scapula: I allow myself to be guided and compelled into deeply inspired action. I feel magnificent, infinite inspiration, and I know how to act on it.

Tap under your arm: I allow infinite intelligence to guide my choices. My choices are smarter, more and more prosperous every day.

Tap on the top of your head. My decisions, inspired by infinite intelligence, are lucky, they take me to prosperous places, they take me to prosperity. I often find myself at the right place and right time.

Tap on your third eye: I allow and trust infinite intelligence to guide me into reaching for goals that are right

Day 16 - You open up for greater inspiration

for me, that bring me the prosperity I want, the fulfillment I want.

Tap on the side of your eye: I relax and trust the universe to inspire me, to guide me, to direct me.

Tap under your eye: I feel active and inspired, and act on ideas from infinite intelligence.

Tap under your nose: I feel like more and more my life is guided into more prosperity, I'm being compelled into prosperous directions.

Tap on your chin: It feels great to be so magnificently inspired, to feel so magnificently encouraged, receive so many magnificent ideas.

Tap on your collarbone: I accept and act on infinite, omniscient intelligence and inspiration, and it feels great to count on such a powerful ally.

Tap on your scapula: Everyday I feel more and more inspired, with clearer goals, making better and better choices, attracting infinite prosperity into my life, tapping into infinite wisdom.

Tap under your arm: I choose to work in line with infinite wisdom, and I trust this powerful guidance. I fine tune my intuition and let it guide me into prosperity.

Tap on the top of your head. My mind opens to amazing ideas, amazing inspiration and it feels great to be connected with this infinite intelligence.

Now take a deep breath. Feel how you're guided and protected. Be open for bursts of inspiration, clearer ideas, and intuition.

This is it for today. Again, always send love to prosperity when you see it. You can also repeat a guided meditation if you like it. Again, before sleeping, set the intention to decide your true prosperity goal for your life.

Summary

Main idea: Being attuned to intuition and your infinite intelligence is a key component to reaching prosperity, since it so often depends on good ideas and smart decisions.

Exercises:

- Tapping 3
- Before sleeping, set the intention to receive guidance for a true goal for two years from now.
- Send love to prosperity when you see it.
- See yourself surrounded with prosperous energy and send it to at least one place or person.
- Avoid complaining.

DAY 17 - YOU ARE LOVED AND GUIDED

Today we're going to continue with the idea of allowing a higher intelligence to guide and inspire you, and we'll do a guided meditation. Yay, finally! New guided meditation!

I also want you to start thinking about a goal for two years from now during the day. It can be specific, like success in a specific business or line of work, but doesn't need to be super specific. Think about an average income you'd like to make. Make sure that it's something you believe is attainable.

There are examples of highly successful people in all lines of business, so maybe use one of those people for inspiration. If you still don't know what you want, it's fine. Don't rush it. The idea is for you to ask for higher intelligence to guide you in choosing an ideal goal for you.

Don't pick your goal yet. If you want a goal for more than two years from now, it's good, too. Make sure it's a life goal, because you should always focus on your real goal, not on the steps to get there.

Today, as always, send love to prosperity when it catches your attention, and imbue something with prosperous, loving energy. You can also repeat the tapping from yesterday, as it will help you open up for higher intelligence.

The meditation for today (Meditation 9) is for you to imagine yourself being loved and protected, and to imagine yourself receiving higher knowledge.

For this, you'll imagine a place of knowledge. It can be a library or a temple. I think it's cool to imagine a library in the clouds, or something magical like that. You'll also imagine a higher being. It can be your higher self, so it would be yourself, just wiser, more powerful, etc. It can be your version of God, and it can be a completely imagined person that represents the wisdom of the Universe. You are going to hug this person, so keep that in mind.

So let's go.

Lie down or sit comfortably. Feel your breath in and out. Breathe, in, in, in, in, hold it, then out, out, out, out, out. Breathe, in, in, in, in, hold it, then out, out, out, out, out.

Day 17 - *You are loved and guided*

Feel how you're connected with the world around you, how the universe permeates your body through air. Imagine now the stars in the universe, the billions of stars, and the greatness and wisdom keeping it all together.

Imagine you're breathing this wisdom with the energy of the stars. Breathe in and out slowly, then feel it moving through your body, relaxing, cleaning, inspiring, from your chest, to your tummy, legs, feet, then up to your back, shoulders, arms, hands, back to your shoulder, neck, and throat.

Feel this energy cleansing and permetating your throat and vocal chords, imbuing your communication with wisdom. Now feel it in your head. Feel how this energy allows your thoughts to become clearer, allow your mind to vibrate in line with prosperity and wisdom.

Now imagine you're going up a set of stairs. You're going to the higher place of knowledge. Feel that you'regoing up some steps. Look at that place, what it contains. It has wisdom and knowledge from the universe. It knows past, future. It's infinite, omniscient. All this knowledge is available to you.

Now imagine a higher being from this place of knowledge. This higher being is going to give you a hug and tell you they love you. You feel loved, secure, protected. Feel that love from the higher being to you. You are a magnificent child of the universe, unique, with your own path to thread, and your own voice to the world. Feel that hug.

Now the higher being is going to take you to a special place in that palace of knowledge. It's a transparent chamber with floating sparkles. Those sparkles represent the wisdom of that palace of knowledge. Your higher being opens the door to you and you enter this chamber.

You can breathe this sparkly energy. It inspires you. It also permeates and penetrates your body and energetic field. You feel the wisdom, inspiration, knowledge, intuition from the universe in your life, in your body, in your mind. You feel that energy cleansing old patterns, resistance, fear. You relax and enjoy your time receiving that wise energy.

Now you go out of the chamber, hug again your higher being, and go back down the stairs.

Feel yourself back in the physical place where you were. Visualize that energy around you. Feel guided and protected. Feel how it gives you inspiration, confidence, wisdom. Feel how it opens you up for intuition and higher ideas.

Feel that energy around you.

Open your eyes. The energy is still with you, and you have the wisdom of the universe to guide you.

. . .

From now on, whenever you have to act on a creative project, or maybe come to a decision, take deep breaths and visualize that energy inspiring you towards smarter decisions, more prosperity and better ideas.

So this was the meditation for today. Learn to use the quick visualization technique whenever you need to have good ideas. If you sit to write, for example, do this before you start. That way you call inspiration to you. It's still possible that you might still feel blocked, or that you'll still write and think everything is crap, but try to hang on to that feeling of higher inspiration, higher knowledge, higher ideas to help you. You can also use it if you have to do a test, or in any other situations when inspiration, wisdom, and knowledge would be welcome.

Don't forget to keep sending loving energy to prosperity when you see it. It's also a good idea to repeat the tapping about allowing a higher intelligence to guide you.

Summary

Main idea: We're continuing to connect with infinite intelligence, intuition, higher knowledge.

Exercises:

- During the day, try to think about a real prosperity goal for about two years from now, something you believe you can attain.
- Do guided meditation 9.
- Send love to prosperity when it catches your eye.
- Surround yourself with prosperous energy and send it to at least one place or one person.
- Avoid complaining.

DAY 18 - YOU EXPAND YOUR IDEA OF PROSPERITY

So I still want you to think about what you want, what you really, really want for two years from now.

I told you it needs to be something you believe you can achieve. Now you may say, "but isn't everything possible? I could set anything as a goal." Sure. But it must be something that your mind can comprehend and absorb. It must be something that fits your ideas of what you can have. Yes, you can start doing affirmations or set a goal to be a billionaire in one year or even one month, even if you barely make minimum wage now. Absolutely!

But if you don't believe it's something you can achieve, you'll have some contrasting vibrations and feelings that will make the manifestation difficult. Manifesting should be easy. It is easy; we manifest crappy things all the time. We just need to embrace better things and enlarge what we believe we deserve and is possible for us. See; you can have anything you want. True, but the sentence is incomplete. You can have anything you want—as long as your mind can encompass that and it matches your energy.

So what are we going to work on? We'll work on your belief, on what you think you can have. A lot of the meditations and tapping should have already opened up your mind for more prosperity, but we're going to work directly on that.

See, some of us have spent years and years with a certain imaginary ceiling that we have difficulty getting past. Those are some deep ingrained feelings and beliefs. Just doing affirmations or visualizations might not be enough to counter that. So what are we going to do? Tapping. Remember how tapping can work on deeply stored feelings and beliefs? So that's what we're going to do today. If you still haven't done tapping, it might be a good time to give it a try. It's awesome. The focus is on expanding our limits, expanding our beliefs of what we can achieve. It's tapping 4.

So let's go to the tapping.

Tap on your karate chop: Today I choose to expand my idea of prosperity, expand my belief of what I can do, achieve, or have. I choose to release any feelings or beliefs in limitations, that I'm not good enough, that I'm unworthy, or that I should settle for less. I choose to release those thoughts, beliefs and feelings from my life, mind, body, and energetic field, from now and forever. Still, I deeply and completely forgive, love, appreciate, and accept myself. I appreciate the fullness of who I am, where my journey has brought me, and where it's leading me. I learn from the past, appreciate what I've learned, and I'm ready to move on with a new outlook in life and new, better-serving beliefs about myself and what I can achieve.

Tap on your third eye: I choose to expand my beliefs about the prosperity I can achieve. I feel my idea of prosperity expanding, and it feels good.

Tap on the side of your eye: I choose to let go of any limiting beliefs, thoughts, feelings about prosperity. I release them from my body, mind, spirit, and energetic field now and forever.

Tap under your eye: I choose to believe in an infinite universe, and believe that I can connect with the fullness of its power and wisdom.

Tap under your nose: I increase, in my mind, the income I can have. I let it increase, increase, increase. I see it increasing in my bank statement, and it feels good.

Tap on your chin: It feels good to feel this increase, expansion, increase in prosperity, expansion in abundance, this feeling of plenty.

Tap on your collarbone: I know deeply and completely

that I am worthy and deserving, and I am worthy of this expansion of prosperity.

Tap on your scapula: I allow my mind to encompass more, believe I deserve and can achieve more, believe in my infinite worth, believe in my connection to the infinite power of the universe.

Tap under your arm: I release any blocks, fears or limitations about the prosperity I can achieve and allow my natural prosperity to flow through me.

Tap on the top of your head: Prosperity allows me to share prosperity, increase prosperity around me, and spread love. I enjoy spreading more and more prosperity around me.

Tap on your third eye: I embrace the prosperity and abundance of the universe. It's infinite, limitless, powerful. It feels good to embrace it.

Tap on the side of your eye: I allow more and more abundance, more and more prosperity, more and more money into my life and the lives of people around me.

Tap under your eye: I am worthy and deserving, and I can see my income growing and growing. It feels good, it feels natural to allow it to grow. I see higher and higher amounts on my bank statement.

Tap under your nose: The more I earn, the more I can

spread prosperity around me, the more good I can do I feel happy and thankful to do more and more good.

Tap on your chin: I'm worthy and deserving of high amounts of money, and I open myself for higher and higher amounts. I see higher and higher amounts in my life.

Tap on your collarbone: I'm worthy and deserving of amazing prosperity. I'm the one who decides its limits, and I choose to expand those limits.

Tap on your scapula: More and more I see myself as rich, prosperous, successful, achieving. More and More I see that it's my true nature. I see this prosperity increasing, I feel that I can be more and more successful.

Tap under your arm: Any blocks, fears, limitations, or negative feelings are released from my life, my experience, and my energetic field now and forever.

Tap on the top of your head: It feels good to allow more and more. It feels good to expand. It feels good to see my prosperity increase and increase and increase.

Take a deep breath.

Feel how your feeling of prosperity, your beliefs of how much you can earn have expanded.

So this is it for today. What else should you do? Well,

again, whenever you see prosperity, send it love. Try to think about what you want in two years from now. You can ask for guidance before sleeping. Do one guided meditation if you have the time.

Summary

Main idea: Your goal needs to be something you believe you can achieve, and expanding your beliefs can help you set bigger, more prosperous goals and still believe in them.

Exercises:

- Tapping 4
- Spend some time thinking about your goal for two years from now. You can also set the intention to receive guidance before sleeping.
- Send love to prosperity when you see it.
- Surround yourself with sparkly, prosperous energy at least once and send it so at least one person or place.

DAY 19 - YOU VISUALIZE YOUR IDEAL GOAL

So today is the day we set or goals! I want you to think about you want for your life. What you really, really want.

Based on that, I want you to have a goal for two years from now. In some cases it can be longer, let's say if you want to be a heart surgeon, but you're only starting university. Sure, set your goal for later. In general, though, I think two years is a good time to set things in motion and achieve what you want in life. Since we've been working on prosperity only, this goal should be prosperity related.

Imagine how much money you are making, where you are living, and what you are doing. Do you need to be specific in what you are doing? I'd say no. Imagine yourself performing your ideal job, for example, and being recognized in it. Don't imagine exactly where you are working.

Make sure you believe this goal is attainable. If you imagine yourself in a certain line of business, there should be enough evidence that it's possible to make x amount per month in that line of business. You must believe in it with your conscious mind. You don't need to plan how you're going to get there yet, but you need to believe it, and then state your goal.

For example, for me I stated that I wanted to be a successful writer, earning ten thousand dollars a month. There are tons and tons of writers making that kind of money and even more, so I knew it was possible. Why didn't I wish for more, then? Because I felt that this was what I could achieve in such a short period, according to my beliefs. I didn't specify if I would be solely independent or with a publisher because those details don't matter. I just saw myself spending my time writing, creating, and earning an amount that would make my life more comfortable.

So in your case, if you want a type of job, imagine yourself working and then seeing your income. If you want a business, see yourself managing it, etc.

I know that some people have no idea how they will reach their prosperity. In this case, imagine only the prosperity, and keep seeking guidance on how you're going to achieve it. Eventually, the answers will come. On the other hand, don't be afraid to imagine something that's not perfect or that you aren't one hundred percent sure. It's always good to move toward a goal, even if you'll call it a crappy goal in the future. It means you're expanding, you have a direction.

So try to pick a goal. Don't be too specific.

So today imagine your prosperity and the kind of activity you are doing, if you know what it is.

For the visualization (visualization 2), you must be awake and sitting. This is less like daydreaming, like we did in the meditations, and more like seeing yourself in the future. It's important to focus on the feelings, so that you feel what you will feel in that situation. Conjure the feeling of being in that situation. It's super important!

Let's go for the visualization. Sit down with your spine straight, and put your hands with palms facing up. Take a slow, deep breath. Breathe in, in, in, then out. Keep breathing slowly, notice how you feel more relaxed, calm, how your thoughts get clearer. Now close your eyes. Feel some of the loving energy we practiced. Feel the prosperous light around you.

it's now two years from now, and you're doing what you decided you want to do, and with the income you want. See yourself performing your duties or taking care of your company. Focus on your feeling of accomplishment, success. Feel how you feel competent and appreciated. Feel how you enjoy your work.

Now let's take a look at your bank account or other place where you can see your income, like an income statement. See yourself looking at it. Feel happy for that amount of money. See yourself looking at it, appreciating it. See the income or amount you've made for yourself. See the kind of clothes you're wearing, the kind of place you live, and more details about your life.

Now say, "This reality, or even better, is in my life now."

That's it! I know that it's two years from now, but the idea is that it's already planted, on its way to manifesting. Energetically, it's already a reality in your life. After this visualization, relax and don't focus too much on it. You can repeat it once a week or once a month, but don't overdo it.

So for today, other than this visualization you can repeat the meditation from yesterday or the tapping for guidance from infinite intelligence. Like always, send love to prosperity, and send prosperous thoughts to places, people, and objects.

Summary

Main idea: Today you'll pick a goal for what you really want in life, for about two years from now. It doesn't need to be perfect or too precise, but you must believe that it's attainable.

Exercises:

- Pick a goal.
- Do Visualization 2 and see your goal achieved.
- Send love to prosperity when you see it.
- Feel yourself surrounded with prosperous energy at least once and send it to at least one person or place.
- Avoid complaining

DAY 20 - SUCCESS IS LOVE MATERIALIZED

When people talk about success, sometimes they think about it as being appreciated and admired, and being successful as something that feeds the ego. Well, yes, but in truth, no. Real success is not selfish or egocentric. Real success is about giving, about allowing other people to have better or more convenient things, entertainment, stuff that they love.

A successful business person creates or sell products or services that people love. A successful artist creates products that people love. A successful employee helps the company run well, helps other people achieve prosperity. Success, true success, is about giving, not about feeding the ego.

You could argue that there are some successful celebrities, for example, that don't do anything. True, but people love to watch them! They provide charisma. The audience feels somehow connected to them, or identifies with them. That's a type of love. The audience loves them, and love is a positive feeling!

I'm a writer, and one thing that can help a writer to be successful is to write to market. Writing to market means writing books people want to read. At first, you might think that writing to market means selling yourself, but if you think about it, it means writing for readers. Writing with love for readers, writing things people will love. Yes, some writers jump on trends hoping to make cash quickly, but that doesn't really work. What works is trying to write for readers. Isn't that a type of love? And you'll be successful in fiction if you write books people love. It's love, and success is love materialized.

A nonfiction writer will have a book that truly helps, inspires, or entertains people. That's love. A great speaker will be inspiring. A nice restaurant chain will provide food people love and maybe, through franchising and other business opportunities, will allow more people to reach prosperity. A successful professional performs their work well, and that helps other people.

Can you see that true success is about love? Can you really feel it? Because if you have negative ideas about success, for example, that it's selling out, it's going to be harder for you to be successful. If you feel that success is about feeding the ego, depending on your spiritual sensibility, you'll have trouble being successful. So you need to see the beauty and love present in success, and how successful people, for the most part, spread some kind of love to the world.

Now, of course, some people are successful and don't have a lot of money. Some people have a lot of money and aren't successful, like someone with a high-paying job that makes them miserable—although you could argue that they are professionally successful to some extent.

Still, I really believe that true prosperity is related to some degree of success, and that if you're reading this book, you want not only more money, but also a feeling of plenty, of accomplishment, and success is part of that. At least you want to be successful in your goal for more prosperity, right? And usually more prosperity means you can buy more expensive things, maybe pay people better, and spread prosperity around you. That's a type of love, too.

Today we're going to do a guided visualization (visualization 3) for love and success. You'll have to imagine your work and surround it with love. If you're a creator, just imagine whatever you create, even if it's digital, like a website, digital downloads, videos, etc. If you are a professional, imagine that light of love in your activity. For example, if you're an athlete, see yourself performing your exercise. If you have a business, see the business, like your office or restaurant. If you create or sell something, see your product, and so on.

. . .

Sit comfortably, but with your spine straight, and have your hands with palms up.

Breathe in slowly, very slowly, then out slowly. Breathe in slowly, very slowly, then out slowly again. Feel how your slow breath calms you. You feel centered, calm, serene. Imagine a person, a pet, or a memory that evokes feelings of love on your chest. Feel the warmth of this love in your heart. Feel this love. Feel that it's a light, and that in the invisible world, it's like a beacon. Imagine you can see this light shining from far away, that it's a beacon of love.

Now you're going to imbue your work, your activity, something you create, with that energy of love. Feel that it's brilliant with love, it's also like a beacon. See your work brilliant and energized, magnetic with love.

Now feel this energy of love expanding and reaching out to potential clients or audience. Feel that it's touching the hearts of a lot of people, depending on the potential reach of your activity. Feel that people are being attracted to your work. Feel that people are feeling better, are feeling positive feelings when in the presence of your work.

Feel how your love, through your work, benefits a lot of people. Feel that potential clients or audience feel attracted to your work. Feel that the love in it makes it magnetic.

People who can benefit from your work feel attracted to it, they are directed towards your work, they'll come to your work. Feel how it's attracting people. Now feel how it's spreading love to the world.

Now feel this feeling of love in your chest. Feel the good feeling of sending love to other people. It feels good to give. You feel accomplished, happy, successful. You're happy to spread love. You're happy to help the world increase its vibrations. Feel the immensity and power of the love flowing through you to your work and to other people. Feel how it warms your heart, how it makes you feel good.

Now open your eyes. Feel that love with you.

This is it. From now on, whenever you send something related to work, whenever you create something, imbue it with this loving energy, and feel it spreading love to anyone who might benefit from it. I know we did the loving prosperity earlier, which is also great, but you can send it to anything or anyone, not necessarily just your work.

This time it's more about your own work or profession, and you also imagine it reaching out to people's hearts and attracting people to your work.

This is the visualization for today.

As always, whenever you see prosperity, send it love! Also, send loving, prosperous energy to other people and places.

Summary

Main idea: Success means you're creating, selling or doing something people love. It's people's love for something that creates success. That means you should enjoy sending love in your world, and appreciate success as a manifestation of that love.

Exercises:

- Visualization 4
- Send love to prosperity.
- Feel yourself surrounded by prosperous light and send it to at least one person or place.
- Avoid complaining.

DAY 21 - YOU LOVE SUCCESS

Today we're going to work a little more on the feeling and idea of success. One thing that's also important for you to do is not to have negative feelings when you see someone who's successful. You need to identify with them. So, the same way you sent love to prosperity, send love to success when it catches your eye, especially if you feel a little tug of envy or negative feelings. Counter it with love!

What if they didn't do anything to deserve that success? You should still appreciate it. If you have negative feelings when you see someone who achieved success easily, without struggle, your subconscious will notice and absorb that idea.

It writes down: okey dokey, success with struggle = good, easy success = bad.

You can see how that is going to help you.

Today we're going to do a tapping session for you to feel successful and feel that you can have success in your endeavors. It's also meant to get rid of any resistance against success. It's tapping 5.

Let's go:

Tap on your karate chop: Today I'm opening myself to success, to feelings of success, to a true belief that I can be successful in all my endeavors. I deeply and completely appreciate, love, and forgive the fullness of who I am and the path that brought me to this moment. I'm ready for new, more and more successful heights, and it feels great to be ready.

Tap on your third eye: I open up for success. I open up for success to enter my life.

Tap on the side of your eye: I allow success in my life. I know I deserve success, I'm worthy of success.

Tap under your eye: I connect to the higher intelligence of the universe, and it allows me to have success and spread this wisdom and love to the world.

Tap under your nose: I feel the energy of success more

and more present in my life, my thoughts. I'm inspired towards success, I act towards success.

Tap on your chin: It feels good to recognize that I can be successful, that I can let the magnificence of my being shine a light in the world.

Tap on your collarbone: It feels great to allow success, to flow with the energy of success, and let it guide me.

Tap on your scapula: Success is something that is good for the people around me and good to the world. My success spreads joy and love.

Tap under your arm: It feels great to feel deeply that I am worthy of great success. I feel excited and eager to spread love to the world.

Tap on the top of your head: Opening up and allowing success feels natural to me. It feels good to allow more and more success.

Tap on your third eye: I allow the energy of success to permeate my thoughts, my actions, my vibration, and it feels so good, I allow it more and more.

Tap on the side of your eye: I feel the energy of success in my energetic field. It goes with me wherever I go, a bright beacon of love. It feels so good!

Tap under your eye: I allow my heart to open up and expand, and transform unconditional, universal love in success, spreading love to the world. So much love!

Tap under your nose: I feel successful, I think successful thoughts, I make successful actions, I aim for successful goals.

Tap on your chin: I am connected to the wisdom of the universe, and I am confident that I have all it takes to achieve great heights.

Tap on your collarbone: I let go of any need to block, resist, or fear my natural path to success. Any resistance has been eliminated from my body, mind, and energetic field now and forever.

Tap on your scapula: I'm so thankful for having the chance to spread love to the world, to achieve my plein potential, to reach success in my endeavors.

Tap under your arm: My natural path is aimed towards success, and it feels good to be in line with my magnificent, true nature.

Tap on the top of your head: I allow myself to shine. My light is good for the world.

Now take a deep breath.

You should feel a lot more confident and successful!

This is a great tapping exercise to do before a job interview, for example.

This is the exercise for today. You can repeat any of the

guided meditations if you have the time. Also, it's a good idea to repeat the visualization of your true, real goal, especially now that you have raised your success consciousness. Don't forget to send love to prosperity and success when it catches your eye.

Summary

Main idea: it's important to appreciate success when you see it and identify with success.

Exercises

- Tapping 5
- Send love to prosperity and success when you see it
- At least once a day, send love to your work and imagine that love attracting potential clients.
- Surround yourself with prosperous energy at least once and send it to at least one person or place.

DAY 22 - YOU CARRY A LUCKY STAR

Three weeks have passed. Yay! You may have noticed that we covered many elements that can contribute to prosperity. One factor that everyone mentions that we only covered in part is luck.

Yes, being connected with your intuition and feeling aligned with prosperity in itself already helps a lot with luck. You might find yourself at the right place and right time not because of some randomness of the universe, but because you are connected to a higher intelligence guiding you.

Beyond that, though, it's a good idea to practice feelings of luck as in random luck. You see, if you want to manifest things, sometimes they come in weird ways we can't explain. We call it luck. Our logical mind calls it luck. It can be the synchronicity of the universe, but since we call it luck, let's run with it! Just believing that you're lucky can have a huge impact on your vibration.

Today we'll do a guided meditation. It's guided meditation 10.

Sit or lie down comfortably, and relax in the way you prefer, like using the light and having it relax your entire body. Also have a feeling of love in your chest. It helps a lot.

Now you're going to imagine you're going up the stairs to the temple of knowledge. See the place, the details.

Now the higher being is coming to you with a gift. You receive a necklace with a pendant. The pendant is a blue crystal star. You are then told that this is a lucky star, that whenever you wear it you'll be lucky.

You're also told that this star is invisible in the material world, so you can wear it whenever you want. Your higher being tells you to go back and carry the star.

You feel that you are physically where you were before. Feel that you carry the star with you. From now on, whenever you do something that you think would benefit from luck, feel your lucky star pendant. Feel that you are lucky in all your endeavors.

. . .

Now, super caveat here: don't use it to play on the lottery or gamble. Why?

Because lottery or gambling, when they are a habit, usually mean a disconnection from prosperity. The idea that you need to win the lottery to be rich means a belief that you can't build your own prosperity, that your prosperity doesn't come from you.

I've also noticed that a lot of people who constantly play the lottery don't have strong feelings of prosperity, and it's probably not a coincidence.

Now you may say, "But hey, I can get whatever I want, and I'm lucky, why not win the lottery?"

I'll tell you another reason; it's one more crappy goal. Yeah, crappy. They come in all shapes and sizes. Why is it crappy? Because you are limiting the way you'll receive prosperity by focusing on the lottery and because what you really want is a life of abundance and fulfillment, and oftentimes winning a large amount doesn't provide that.

I have an aunt who actually won the lottery. She told me she visualised herself waking up the steps to receive the prize at the lottery office. See? It works.

But.

She won one hundred thousand dollars. Don't laugh, it was some twenty years ago and it was a lot more money then. Also, it was probably within what she was capable of attracting.

Do you want to guess what happened? Well, she spent the money then went back to a life of limited prosperity. It wasn't bad, but wasn't ideal either.

What I'm here thinking is that if she could use the law of attraction and visualization to win the lottery, she could have used it to imagine a constant stream of prosperity in her life. It might have been better. So this is one reason why I don't recommend focusing on the lottery.

Another reason is that it's hard. See, with prosperity, all the steps are logical. You can obviously make money if you provide a good service or product that people love or if people love you. There isn't any resistance in our minds. We know it makes sense, it's just a matter of getting there. Now, for lottery, it's harder. Anyway, you're free to do what you want, but I would really love it if you used your luck for awesome, lasting things for you.

So feel and believe that you're lucky. Feel your lucky star, and go on to your projects, meetings, and more with all the confidence you need.

This is it for today. You can also repeat your goal visualization.

Summary

Main idea: believing in luck is good, and it's good to feel in line with energies of luck. Don't gamble or bet on the lottery, though. Believing that you need the lottery for prosperity means a lack of belief in your own abilities.

Exercises:

- Meditation 10
- Send love to prosperity and success when it catches your attention.
- Send love to your work and see how it attracts clients.
- Feel prosperous energy around you and send it to someone.
- Avoid complaining.

DAY 23 - YOU LOVE LUCK!

Today we're going to continue working on feeling lucky. Something that's important to pay attention now is how you react when you see somebody who's lucky. Do you feel a tug of envy, do you think they are hacks who don't deserve what they have? it's a common feeling.

Lots of people feel that if someone achieves a goal due to luck, they're unworthy of that goal, or they feel that achieving things due to luck is not a valid way of achieving them.

But it's not true. If everything is energy, being lucky means you're aligned with whatever you achieved! Luck might be a name we give to fast manifestation we can't explain.

And again, negative feelings when you see someone who got money or whatever by sheer luck makes your subconscious think that luck is a bad, shameful thing, something you don't want, something you should avoid.

Either way, it doesn't matter why some people are lucky or not. Remember you have your magical lucky star, so you should feel identification with people who are lucky, and lucky situations. Whenever you see someone who got something because of luck, send love to this luck. Send love to luck, feel love when you see luck, and identify with lucky people.

Other than that, today we're going to do a tapping session to hold onto those feelings of luck. It's tapping 6.

Tap on your karate chop: Today I choose to open myself for luck. Pure luck. Why not? Luck is only a manifestation of my energy, my alignment. I choose to be aligned with prosperity, and therefore I attract luck and I deserve it.

Tap on your third eye: I open myself for luck. Luck is good, luck is fun, and I open up for it.

Tap on the side of your eye: I align with prosperity and abundance, and this alignment brings me a lot of luck.

Tap under your eye: I'm worthy and deserving of being lucky. I am worthy of seeing things working out by themselves, and sometimes achieving things without any effort.

Tap under your nose: it's fine to achieve things, win things, or gain things by pure luck, and I choose to allow luck to help me.

Tap on your chin: I feel great to be lucky. I feel appreciation for so much luck in my life, for how things just magically work out.

Tap on your collarbone: My magical blue lucky star is with me at all times, and it's attracting luck wherever I go, and especially when I remember that I'm super lucky.

Tap on your scapula: It feels so great to allow luck in my life, to see that things flow more smoothly, that things work out well, and sometimes better than expected.

Tap under your arm: Luck is now part of my life. Luck permeates my body, mind, and energetic field. It feels good to be lucky and allow so much luck in my life.

Tap on the top of your head: Luck is fun, luck is good, luck is something that I appreciate. I feel good to be lucky.

Tap on your third eye: I love luck everywhere. I love seeing the universe doing its magic just because. I love being in line with this energy.

Tap on the side of your eye: I love seeing people get

lucky. It's great for them and I'm happy for them. It feels good to see luck.

Tap under your eye: Getting lucky is a valid way to reach my goals. I allow it because I deserve it.

Tap under your nose: Luck is the name people give to fast manifestation they don't understand. I like fast manifestation therefore I like luck.

Tap on your chin: Being lucky is fun and I enjoy it. It feels great to see the universe in action, making things easy for me, and even bringing me surprises.

Tap on your collarbone: My lucky star is always with me, bringing me luck, making things work out easily, helping me when things seem random.

Tap on your scapula: It feels good to allow luck, to allow the universe to work its magic in my life. I feel luck all around me, I feel lucky energy, and I see lucky results.

Tap under your arm: Luck permeates my body, mind, and energetic field. I'm surrounded by luck, I project luck, I expect luck, and I get luck.

Tap on the top of your head: It feels good to allow luck in my life, and allow its magic to bring me prosperity easily.

This is it for today. Send love to prosperity when you see

it, and also to success and luck. You were probably already doing it, since a lot of it is prosperity, but it's good to be aware of that. You can repeat any guided meditation. Something else you might want to do is start thinking about a short-term prosperity goal, like for a month or so from now.

Summary

Main idea: it's a good idea to identify with lucky people and situations.

Exercises:

- Tapping 6
- Send love to prosperity, success, and luck when it catches your attention.
- Surround yourself with prosperous energy and send it to at least one person or place.
- Surround your work with love and feel it attracting clients.
- Think about a prosperity goal for one month from now

DAY 24 - YOU VISUALIZE PROSPERITY IN YOUR NEXT MONTH

All right. At this point you might be saying, "Well, it's all nice and neat, but I need money NOW." Well, in truth, a lot of the previous exercises should have helped you attract better opportunities. Still, like we did with the long-term goal, we're also going to visualize a short-term goal for prosperity. But there are rules.

Rule number one: it must not contradict or hinder your ideal goal. See? That's why we left this for later.

Once you know what you really want, what you truly want, your short-term goals must be in line with it. And it's fine if you aren't that prosperous right now. Lots of people have to go through difficult periods when working on something bigger. Sometimes you have to invest unpaid time and even money. Right.

That said, it doesn't mean you can't wish for more prosperity. See, maybe your big goal requires you to work only part time, for example, but maybe you can attract a better job. And it's fine to consider your immediate prosperity. Just make sure you don't sacrifice your true goals.

Rule number two: no more crappy goals. Wow, wow, wow, you may say. It has to be a crappy goal, right? Since it's just to make money while working for the big goal. Well, my point is: don't limit it. In some cases, you can even leave out the how, and just trust the universe to bring you the right answer. You can imagine your occupation, but try not to limit it by choosing exactly how it's going to manifest.

You'll do a visualization and imagine yourself in one month, with the income you think you can achieve in that period and that doesn't interfere with your big goal. Here, again, you need to believe in your goal. It's visualization 4.

So let's go.

Sit down with your spine straight and hands with the palms up, and close your eyes. Take a slow, deep breath. Breathe in, in, in, in, hold it, hold it, then out, out, out, out, out. Breathe in, in, in, in, hold it, hold it, then out, out, out, out, out.

Feel that you're connected with a golden energy of prosperity from the universe. Just quiet your mind and feel this connection. See yourself in one month. See your bank account, or anything tangible where you can see your prosperity. Feel satisfied, calm, happy about it. Imagine how you feel about it. See yourself in the scene. Feel how it's a reality. Now say: This or better is a reality in my life.

Take a deep breath and let it go. It's sent to the universe.

This is it for today. You can repeat any tapping or guided meditation, and send love to prosperity, success, and luck when you see it.

Summary

Main idea: it's good to have prosperity soon, too. as long as it doesn't clash with your main goal.

Exercises:

- Pick a goal for your more immediate future that doesn't hinder your bigger goal.
- Visualization 4
- Send love to prosperity, love, and success when you see it.

- At least once, surround yourself with prosperous energy, and send it to at least one person or place.
- Surround your work with love and feel how it attracts clients.
- Avoid complaining.

DAY 25 - YOU ALLOW UNEXPECTED PROSPERITY

All right. So you have everything set up for your big goal. You're connected to wisdom, success, and luck. But you can also open up for extras here and there on the way.

Today we're going to do a visualization.Visualization 5. This is just so you open up for unexpected prosperity.

Sit down with your spine straight and hands with the palms up, and close your eyes. Take a slow, deep breath. Breathe in, in, in, in, hold it, hold it, then out, out, out, out, out. Breathe in, in, in, in, hold it, hold it, then out, out, out, out, out.

Feel that you're connected with a golden energy of prosperity from the universe. Just quiet your mind and feel this connection.

Now see an unexpected, completely unexpected check in your mailbox. You can't see the amount, but you're happy. Touch this check, feel it. Feel the emotion and sensation you feel.

Now see your bank statement or wherever else you can receive money and see an unexpected deposit. Feel what you would feel. You're probably surprised, thankful, excited.

Now say: Thanks universe, for this awesome, unexpected gifts.

Now open your eyes.

This should help you get some unexpected money. You can also do it within a timeframe, but do it and forget. If you keep checking your mailbox or account it doesn't work.

So this is it for today, a little extra while the lessons from the previous day solidify. Today you can repeat any tapping or guided meditation, and send love to prosperity, luck, and success wherever you find it.

Summary

Main idea: it's good to get unexpected money and prosperity, and you can be open for it.

Exercises:

- Visualization 5
- Send love to prosperity, love, and success when you see it.
- At least once, surround yourself with prosperous energy, and send it to at least one person or place.
- Surround your work with love and feel how it attracts clients.
- Avoid complaining.

DAY 26 - YOU TAKE INSPIRED ACTION TOWARDS YOUR TRUE GOALS

All right, we're almost at the end. Since you've already set a big goal, it's time to come back to it, especially now that you should feel more equipped to work towards it.

it's important to commit and act towards your goals. And sometimes there can be challenges, despite all your luck, but if it's something you want, you'll find the strength and resilience, and you'll avoid procrastination, fear, or any other blocks.

Since we're talking about blocks, you know what we're going to do, right? Yes, tapping. This is to help you focus on your goals and to take inspired action towards it. In a way, it also brings together the different skills and mindsets we practiced. This is tapping 7.

. . .

See and feel your goal. See yourself with your goal fulfilled. Now let's tap.

Tap on your karate chop: I have a goal, and it's a great goal, because I am choosing something that aligns with my true self. I choose to focus on my goat and take inspired action towards it. I choose to move towards plenty fulfillment, and prosperity, and I'm doing it without distraction. I choose to love and appreciate the fullness of who I am, and I focus on manifesting the fullness of my potential.

Tap on your third eye: I choose to focus on my true goals, real goals, goals that are good for me, that align with who I am.

Tap on the side of your eye: My effory, energy and thoughts are directed towards things that matter, that will make my life more fulfilling and prosperous.

Tap under your eye: I no longer choose or get distracted with crappy goals. Instead, I'm focused and determined to achieve what I really want.

Tap under your nose: I am deeply inspired and guided by infinite intelligence, and I allow this intelligence to act through me.

Tap on your chin: I'm compelled into inspired action, and it feels good to let this inspiration flow through me.

Tap on your collarbone: I am on the path of achieving

my goals, and it's natural to be on this path, my true self's path. I feel good in it.

Tap on your scapula: It feels great to allow greater inspiration to direct me towards my goal, to guide me and incite inspired action.

Tap under your arm: I am focused, excited, inspired, and I let go of any resistance or fear about my goal.

Tap on the top of your head: I am worthy and deserving of achieving my true goals, and I know I am capable of achieving them.

Tap on your third eye: I'm aligned with success, and I'll bring success to whatever I set out to do.

Tap on the side of your eye: I'm aligned with luck, and I'll bring this great luck to my goals.

Tap under your eye: I step forward with confidence and grace, knowing that the universe is backing me up and I am ready to reach greater heights.

Tap under your nose: With the wisdom and luck of the universe on my side, I'm unstoppable and I'm using this unstoppable energy towards goals that matter.

Tap on your chin: I love taking deeply inspired action, and seeing my goals getting closer and closer. It feels good to know I can achieve my goals.

Tap on your collarbone: My lucky star is here to help me, and I know it will help me on my way.

Tap on your scapula: it's amazing to know that I have everything I need to achieve what I want and that I'm going in that direction.

Tap under your arm: My body, mind, spirit, and energetic field are aligned with my true goals, and the universe is aligning for it.

Tap on the top of your head: I choose to focus on my goals and bring huge prosperity for my life.

Take a deep breath.

That's it. If you have something you need to work towards, it's good to be focused and determined, and this tapping really helps. Speaking about your goal, try to visualize it once every week.

You can repeat a meditation today. Don't forget to send love to prosperity, luck, and success when you see it!

Summary

Main idea: Focus on your goal again.

Exercises:

Day 26 - You take inspired action towards your true goals

- Tapping 7
- Send love to prosperity, success and luck when it catches your attention.
- At least once, surround yourself with prosperous energy, and send it to at least one person or place.
- Surround your work with love and feel how it attracts clients.
- Avoid complaining.

DAY 27 - TIME TO PUT IT IN ACTION

Okay, so we've done all that and your energy should have shifted a lot. Now it's time to put your prosperity goal in action.

What concrete steps can you take to achieve it? Try to think. If you don't know, try to do some research. Find out what you need to do. Learn how to do well whatever you set out to do.

Now you may say, "But wait, aren't those the crappy goals?" Yes and no. Steps along the way are necessary. As long as you recognize them as steps, and keep the real goal in mind, you'll be fine. The problem is when you get so involved in a step that you forget why you're taking it and where you really want to go. Plus, we all need signposts, directions towards where to go, and it's good to be guided to your goal.

So try to plan what you need to do to achieve your real goal. You might have to do some sacrifices, and you'll probably face some failures along the way. It's all fine. As long as you learn from the obstacles and keep moving forward, you're good, and they're not really failures.

How can you plan? You can set it in writing. It's fine if you start just by the first steps, but sometimes it's important to reverse engineer.

See the result, and then how to get there. The reason is that sometimes we make wrong assumptions about how to reach a goal. Connecting with your inner guidance should help, but you can always do your own research. You can also ask people who are more successful than you. Surprisingly, people like to help, and they could answer a few questions.

Either way, find a method to understand what steps you need to take, so that you have a sense of direction. You're still open to your intuition, and changes might happen, but it's important that you get motivated to walk towards your goal.

And now you may also ask: why action? Can't we just turn thoughts into prosperity? I'll say that this is a universe of action. We eat three times a day, meaning that in our natural state, in nature, we need to do something every day. Your thoughts allow you to be aligned with prosperity, to have better desires, to expand the possibilities, but you if your actions aren't aligned with your thoughts, something's wrong. Well, actually, actions are always aligned with thoughts. We can't split ourselves in two.

Also, we're in a universe of action. You wake up and do something. Yes, this something can be watching TV or scrolling through social media, but you are certainly doing something at all times. So acting towards your goal means **focusing your actions** towards your goals.

You're going to act regardless. If your actions are not in line with your thoughts, there is usually some discrepancy or disharmony. Plus, your thoughts follow your actions. You can't possibly be scrolling through social media while at the same time thinking about achieving a goal.

Right, there's another kind of non-action; reading about your goal. Getting informed is good and super important, but it's possible to get caught up in it, and keep reading, reading, getting more and more informed, participating in groups, and not acting towards your goal. It's possible to get caught in the planning and research stage. Don't do it. Move towards it. Action causes alignment, and you learn better through action. Acting towards our dreams makes us happy, even if we look back and think that those were crappy dreams. It's what life is for.

So how do you do it? Visualize your goal, plan steps to achieve it, and make sure you're following those steps. Have a plan of action, even if it's flexible. Feel that you're moving towards your goal. If you still don't know how to achieve it, take some time to research and learn, then make your plan.

I know that some books, like *Think and Grow Rich*, tell you to write down your goal and read it every day. You can do it if you want.

The point is for you to know where you are going. If you read it every day, make sure you don't make a big deal out of it. If you think you have to conjure faith or belief, it means that the goal is not within what your mind can encompass.

Maybe you should scale down your goal a bit, so that your goal seems more possible, or you can also work on expanding your beliefs.

Remember: your mind needs to encompass your goal. In your mind, in your energy, it needs to be a normal reality, not a wish, a dream, a miracle. It needs to be present and feel natural. The exercises in this book should help you.

And if you read your goal every day, a good trick is to send loving energy to it, then visualize yourself in detail doing it and how you feel doing it. Regardless of how you wish to keep your goal in mind, make sure you do it and keep focused. You can also do the tapping for your goal, and your goal visualization, or do all three, but keep your goal in mind, again, just making sure you feel relaxed and not that you're trying to achieve something impossible. If you can achieve it, it's possible, if it's impossible, you can't achieve it.

You're competent and can do something that people love, so reaching success should be a natural consequence of your actions.

And what if you fail? It means you're trying. Learn with it, adapt, and move on. Keep going. Accepting "failure" and rejection and moving on is often the difference between achievers and quitters. And it's not failure if you're still trying.

So this is it for today. We're reaching the end. It's a very good idea to repeat the tapping to focus on your goal today, and get ready for tomorrow, when we wrap it up.

Summary

Main idea: Keep your main goal in mind in your future

Exercises:

- Send love to prosperity, success and luck when it catches your attention.
- At least once, surround yourself with prosperous energy, and send it to at least one person or place.

- Surround your work with love and feel how it attracts clients.
- Avoid complaining.
- Plan your next steps to reaching your goal.
- From now on, it's a good idea to keep your goal in mind. You can do the tapping for your goal, the visualization, or even write down your goal. Just make sure that when you focus on your goal you see it as something achievable and normal.

DAY 28 - YOU KEEP PROSPEROUS THOUGHTS FOR LIFE

All right. So this is it. If you've followed the exercises, you should feel a difference in the way you think and the way you feel about money. Your work doesn't stop now. Keep doing prosperity meditations, visualizations, and tapping.

I suggest at least two tapping sessions or meditations, and one visualization a week. The guided meditations from the beginning of this book are really powerful. Don't discount them because they are simple. Sometimes, the simpler, the better.

You should turn sending love to prosperity, luck, and success into a habit. See those things as good and feel aligned to them. Continue paying attention to your thoughts, and avoid complaining.

Reach for your goals, and be mindful of true goals versus crappy goals. And hey, crappy goals come in all shapes, incomes, and sizes. A crappy goal could be a higher paying job than your true goal, for example. It could be a goal you had just because you thought it would make you important, or your family wanted, or something of the sort.

Again, crappy goals come in all shapes, monetary values, and sizes. True goals too. Remember to connect with your inner self and keep in touch with it when reaching out for greater achievements.

And ask yourself often: why am I doing what I'm doing? Where is this leading me? Ask. Truly ask. Sometimes we get caught up in things that make us waste our time and lead us nowhere.

So the questions are: Where do I truly want to go? Is this helping?

Hey, sometimes you have to do things that don't necessarily help you go where you want directly, like taking a job to pay the bills, but if you think about it, it helps with your goal because it frees you from some monetary worries.

The issue is if you take a job you don't want, for example, then find yourself working there sixty hours a week. I mean, again, maybe you find that you love that job and change your goal. In this case that's great! Just make sure you ask where your activities are leading you, and where you want to go.

Keep doing meditations. Keep doing tapping. Take fifteen minutes a day for some of these activities. Everything starts with the mind, everything is energy at first, so work on your energy, work on expanding your mind.

Summary

Main idea: Keep working on cultivating a prosperous energy and mindset and reaching towards your true goals.

Exercises **for the rest of your life:**

- Do two mediations, visualizations, or tapping sessions per week. You can do more if you want.
- Send love to prosperity, luck, and success whenever it catches your attention.
- At least once a day, remember to surround yourself with prosperous energy, and send it to at least one person or place.
- Surround your work with love and feel how it attracts clients.

- Avoid complaining.
- Focus on your goals. Remember who you are and what you really want.
- Ask yourself: where do I want to do? Is this helping me?

TALLY AND RECAP - SOME OF WHAT YOU LEARNED

So, in the beginning of this book I've promised you'd learn a few things, right?

Let's go back and recap:

- **No more blaming yourself. Appreciate who you are.**

We did it in out first day, right? Appreciate how prosperous you are. We also did it in the tapping sessions, where you are bringing up negative thoughts, but always start by forgiving and loving yourself and the fullness of who you are.

- A super efficient technique to get rid of envy or negative feelings when you see people who are more successful or prosperous than you.

Yay. You know what it is, right? Send it love! Love to success, love to prosperity, love to luck. Love is such a positive feeling that it will smash any yucky, negative stuff that keeps you from reaching your true prosperity.

- No more crappy goals. Learn the right way to aim for what you truly deserve.

Yes. You should want what you want. And the right way to aim for your goal is to first do some prosperity work, so you're not in a crappy mentality, and also to ask for some guidance and give yourself some time. We did all that. Repeat the process in the future, if you ever want to set a goal.

- Count on your inner guidance to reach for better goals and find prosperity.

The trick is to ask for guidance. If you are the most skeptical of all the skepticals, you should still recognize that stopping and allowing intuition and inner guidance is a good thing. If you believe in something greater, you should know that it makes a lot of sense to let it act through you than to try to tough it out and solve everything on your own. We learned a meditation, a tapping session, and a visualization to help you with that. Sometimes just the intention is not enough, you need to work on your subconscious mind.

- **Learn to love success and attract success.**

I think that success really is love materialized. If you see it as love, you see it as a positive force, and you're ready to allow it in your life. By imbuing your work with love, you're attracting success.

- **Learn to love and attract luck.**

Yay. Same thing. Luck is awesome. Luck means that the universe is bringing stuff to you.

- **The right way to do affirmations so that they don't cause resistance.**

Wow, wow, wow. We didn't do any long sessions on affirmations, right? But that's exactly the point. Affirmations were done while tapping. Tapping gets rid of negative feelings. If you're saying "I attract money" and feeling "I definitely don't attract money", the tapping will help you get rid of that negative feeling. If you do affirmations on your own, make sure you're feeling them and not resisting them.

- **How to reach the right energy to present yourself better in job interviews or when to close business.**

Those meditations where you surrounded yourself in loving light, prosperous light, brilliant light were a lot of fun, right? But guess what they'll do? Improve your energy! That will have an immediate impact in any face-to-face interaction.

- **Make your work magnetic and attractive.**

You surround it with love. It might be just a mental thing, and if you're super skeptical, it at least affects your intention creating the work. If you believe in energy and how our thoughts create things, it's easy to see how a work surrounded with love, aiming to give people love will have much higher chances of success.

- **Set long-term goals after you've done the groundwork in the first days and you'll see a huge difference.**

Yes. That was an important point of the book, to take the time to allow you to state your goals from a position of abundance and to give you time to think about the goals and use your inner guidance.

So, how did that tally up? Still unsure how to do some of those things? You can go back to the meditations, tapping sessions, and visualizations.

FAQ

What if I miss a day?

Continue from where you stopped. Don't skip a day from the book.

Is it a huge problem if I miss a day?

No, of course not. But what if you start missing? It means you won't have the focused work for four weeks, and it might impact your results. If, however, you keep doing the meditations and exercises during those days, there is no problem.

Can I take longer with the book and do a day more than once?

Yes, as long as you keep doing it in order, but I'd say it's not necessary. You'll have opportunities to repeat exercises, so if you think you need a little more of a particular day, you'll be able to repeat it later, within the 28 days.

What if I can't find a goal?

Give yourself more time. Eventually, though, it's important to pick something. It doesn't need to be perfect. Our lives need direction, movement, otherwise time slips by and we don't go anywhere. Indecision can be a manifestation of fear. It's better to move on and then correct the course than to remain where you are and never get anywhere.

What if I change my mind about my goal?

Adjusting and adapting along the way is normal. As long as you're not moving from goal to goal to the point you get paralyzed, you're fine.

And yes, it's fine to decide you're not going on a good direction and change route, but if you're doing it often it might be a symptom of fear, confusion, etc. In this case, do the tapping and meditations for higher guidance, take some time, and try to pick and stick with a goal even if you hate it. Achieving a crappy goal beats achieving nothing every time. So reach out for something.

Is there a limit to the guided meditations?

No. Unless specified, you could do any of those meditations every day, and it would be good for you.

What if I hate an exercise?

Try it, at least. If you hate it after doing it, it could be perhaps that it's something you have to work more. It could also be that the exercise is just not your cup of tea, so you can change it..

Can you guarantee that this book works?

Yes. If you do the exercises, you'll have a more prosperous attitude and thoughts. It will help you choose better goals and perform better in job interviews, for example. You'll also feel less anxious about money.

GUIDED MEDITATIONS

ABOUT GUIDED MEDITATIONS

In the next pages you'll find all the guided meditations in detail, with a longer relaxing intro, so that you can follow them or listen to them.

Guided meditations are meant to work on your subconscious mind, and that's why you have to be in a sort of sleepy or daydreaming state.

Don't worry if you don't sleep during the meditation. As long as you're relaxing and enjoying the experience, it's fine.

Don't worry if you sleep either, unless you're falling asleep during the relaxation when you're doing the meditation on your own. If you're listening to this meditation, it's not a problem if you fall asleep in the beginning because the voice will continue guiding you.

You can do these meditations in bed before sleeping, and it's fine if you fall asleep while doing them. You'll probably continue them in your dreams, which is pretty good.

So basically, there are no hard rules. You can do them on your own, imagining the situations that are described in this book, or you can listen to them. It's your call.

1

SENDING LOVE TO MONEY

THIS MEDITATION IS INCLUDED AND EXPLAINED IN DAY 2.

Sit or lie down comfortably in a quiet place.

Breathe in slowly, slowly breathing in, hold it for a bit, then out slowly, slowly, slowly slowly. Breathe in slowly, slowly breathing in, hold it for a bit, then out slowly, slowly, slowly slowly. Breathe in slowly, slowly breathing in, hold it for a bit, then out slowly, slowly, slowly slowly.

Focus on your breath. Feel this air relaxing you, and this relaxation spreading from your chest to your entire body. This relaxation goes down to your belly, legs, feet, relaxing deeply. You feel this wave of relaxation coming up and relaxing your back, shoulders, arms, hands, neck, throat, and head. You're fully relaxed. Completely relaxed.

Now think about a person or pet who brings you feelings of love, ideally not a romantic partner. It can be a child you love (your child or grandchild), a pet, or maybe a memory of when you were young and felt very loved. Try to bring up positive, loving feelings.

Keep that memory in your mind and notice the warm feeling in your chest. Give it a color, preferably a warm color, like red, pink, or purple. Imagine this is your feeling of love. Love is infinite. Feeling love feels good. You can now feel that energy permeating your entire body and present in your energy field, around you. Feel yourself involved, protected, loved in that energy. Feel that loving energy around you.

Imagine now that you're in a beautiful place in nature. See this beautiful, lovely place. Feel yourself there, physically. Smell the ocean or the leaves, feel the wind, the sun. Feel that you're in this beautiful, relaxing place.

Now imagine you're standing in that beautiful place, and you see a gigantic wooden chest. From your heart, where you had those warm feelings, you take a key and open it. It has so many 100-dollar bills that you know there are many millions there. So many bills! Millions of dollars.

You're going to send your loving energy to that pile of cash. Just send your beautiful energy without expecting anything, without trying to feel anything, without trying to attract, just give freely. Imbue that pile of money with your love. See it surrounded by your love. Feel yourself giving, feeling this positive feeling in relation to that huge amount of money. Feel the pleasure of sending love to that pile of money. Repeat mentally now; "I love money." Truly feel that you love money, while you visualize those loving feelings toward the money.

Repeat again and feel it the best you can: "I love money, I love money." Feel warm feelings towards that huge amount of cash.

Now you can feel yourself back where you were (your chair, your bed), feel yourself surrounded in that loving energy, feeling good. Wherever you go today, whatever you do, you'll have that loving energy with you.

2

SENDING LOVE TO MONEY THEN EMBRACING IT.

THIS MEDITATION IS INCLUDED AND EXPLAINED IN DAY 3.

S it or lie down comfortably in a quiet place.

Breathe in slowly, slowly breathing in, hold it for a bit, then out slowly, slowly, slowly slowly. Breathe in slowly, slowly breathing in, hold it for a bit, then out slowly, slowly, slowly slowly. Breathe in slowly, slowly breathing in, hold it for a bit, then out slowly, slowly, slowly slowly.

Focus on your breath. Feel this air relaxing you. Now think about a person or pet who brings you feelings of love, ideally not a romantic partner. It can be a child you love (your child or grandchild), a pet, or maybe a memory of when you were young and felt very loved. Try to bring up positive, loving feelings.

Keep that memory in your mind and notice the warm

feeling in your chest. Give it a color, preferably a warm color, like red, pink, or purple. Imagine this is your feeling of love. Love is infinite. Feeling love feels good.

See now this loving energy permeating your body. See it going down to your belly, your hips, legs, feet, relaxing your lower body deeply, imbuing it with love. You feel this loving energy coming up and relaxing your back. Feel it penetrating the muscles on your back, relaxing and purifying them deeply. Feel it on shoulders, arms, hands, then back to your shoulders, neck, throat, feel it in your vocal chords face, feel it permeating and illuminating all your facial muscles, then feel it penetrating your head and your thoughts. You're fully relaxed, imbued with loving energy.

You can now feel that energy permeating your entire body and present in your energy field, around you. Feel yourself involved, protected, loved in that energy. Feel that loving energy around you. Imagine again that memory or person that brings you warm feelings of love and feel the warmth in your chest.

Imagine now that you're in a beautiful place in nature. See and feel this beautiful, lovely place. Smell the ocean or the leaves, feel the wind, the sun. Feel that you'rein this beautiful, relaxing place.

Now imagine you're standing in that beautiful place, and you see a gigantic storage chest. From your heart, where you had those warm feelings, you take a key and open it.

It has so many 100-dollar bills that you know there are many millions there. So many bills! Millions of dollars.

You send your loving energy to that pile of cash. Just send your beautiful energy without expecting anything, without trying to feel anything, without trying to attract, just give freely. Imbue that pile of money with your love. See it surrounded by your love. Feel yourself giving, feeling this positive feeling in relation to that huge amount of money. Feel the pleasure of sending love to that pile of money.

Now imagine that your loving energy is transforming the money into energy. See energy where the cash was. See the cash being transformed. It's still money, still the same amount, just in a different form. Imagine it's a very pure, brilliant energy. See this energy, knowing that it's millions of dollars. Now condense that energy in a small, brilliant ball. Since it's imbued with your loving energy, it's magnetically attracted to you. Feel that ball of money energy coming in your direction and entering your chest. Feel that money within you, then its energy permeating your entire body and energetic field. Feel the pleasure of that energy in and around your body, loving money energy. Say: "I embrace the energy of money and I allow it in my energetic field." Field this energy within you.

Now go back to where you are physically. Feel that the energy is with you. It makes you feel good. This energy will be with you wherever you go.

3

BATHING IN GOLDEN, PROSPEROUS LIGHT

THIS MEDITATION IS INTRODUCED AND EXPLAINED IN DAY 5

Sit or lie down in a comfortable place. Now think about the Sun, how powerful it is, how much energy and life it sends to Earth. You receive its rays freely. Imagine that you're receiving this gold light of the sun, and that it's literally gold and prosperity.

Imagine that it's also love from the universe, love that's given to you freely, through the gift of this powerful light. If you believe in God or any other greater force, imagine that this light carries that energy. It's an energy of prosperity, giving, love, energy of Infinite Goodness. Feel that light reaching you.

Feel its power, energy. Feel prosperity in that light. Infinite prosperity from the Universe.

See this golden light relaxing your chest. Breathe in and

out this golden light, slowly. Breathe in, in, in, in, in, hold it, hold it, breathe out, out, out, out, out, out out. Breathe in, in, in, in, in, hold it, hold it, breathe out, out, out, out, out out. Breathe in, in, in, in, in, hold it, hold it, breathe out, out, out, out, out, out out.

It feels good to breathe light. Feel that you're breathing golden, loving, powerful prosperous light. Feel this light relaxing your chest, melting any tension, any knots. Feel how your chest is relaxed and purified. Let this light go down to your stomach, relaxing your organs. Feel how it relaxes you, how it purifies your belly. Let the light relax your hips. Relax.

Feel how this light is cleansing your body. It's cleansing any energy that's not vibrating in accordance with prosperity. It's cleansing and making all cells in your body relax in this infinite light.

See this light going to your legs, penetrating its muscles, relaxing all leg muscles, then your feet. Feel this light massaging deeply your feet. Your feet are brilliant with golden, prosperous light.

Now feel this light coming up your legs to your back. It relaxes and penetrates all your back. It removes tensions, removes old beliefs, old ways of thinking. It deeply relaxes all back muscles. It feels good to have this powerful light on your back, relaxing it.

You feel purified and relaxed. Now feel this light and

energy on your shoulders. They relax, relax, relax. You feel your shoulders absorbing this golden light and relaxing deeply.

Spread this light to your arms and hands. Feel how you can receive this light with your hands. Feel how your hands are brilliant with this powerful, beautiful, prosperous energy. It feels good to have this energy in your hands.

Feel this light go up to your shoulders and neck. It relaxes your neck, relaxes it. The light goes to your throat and vocal chords. See your vocal cords vibrating with this gold, prosperous light, feel your throat brilliant with this beautiful, powerful, light.

Now let it go to your face, relaxing your chin, mouth, tongue, cheeks, jaw, eyes, between your eyes, forehead. Feel this energy relaxing your face deeply. Feel how your face is now brilliant with this energy. It's an energy of prosperity, it's an energy of love. It's positive energy in every muscle in your face. Feel then this energy in your scalp then coming from the tips of your hair or remaining in the scalp. Feel how it's around your head, relaxing your scalp.

Now feel this energy penetrating your mind, your brain, taking over your thoughts. You're opening up for more prosperity, more abundance, more money. Your mind is opening up for richer ideas. You have lovely thoughts, in harmony with your greater good. You're opening up to recognize opportunities, to attract luck and coincidences. You feel good.

Feel how this light is working on your mind, purifying it, filling it with prosperous thoughts. This is a positive light from the universe. Your mind is being programmed to attract and achieve prosperity. Your mind is being programmed with the deep knowledge that you're loved by the universe, and that you're worthy.

Let this golden light penetrate deeply in every cell in your head. Your neurons are now vibrating with this golden light. Your thoughts are becoming sharper, clearer, prosperous. Your thoughts bring you prosperity.

Now feel this light surrounding your entire body. It's a relaxing, golden light. You feel safe, protected, secure. Feel that you're enveloped in this light and that it's love and prosperity from the universe. Feel how it protects you. It feels good to be surrounded and enveloped by this light.

You can now focus on your breathing. Breathe this light in and out, slowly. See how this golden energy is going to spread from your lungs to your entire body. When you're ready, feel your body again. Imagine that it's golden, it's shiny with golden, sparkly energy, attracting abundance. Keep breathing this light slowly until you're ready to get up.

4

FIRST VISIT TO YOUR ABUNDANCE CASTLE

THIS MEDITATION IS INTRODUCED AND EXPLAINED IN DAY 6.

Sit or lie down in a comfortable place. Now think about the Sun, how powerful it is, how much energy and life it sends to Earth. You receive its rays freely. Imagine that you're receiving this gold light of the sun, and that it's literally love from the universe, transformed in gold and prosperity. If you believe in God or any other greater force, imagine that this light carries that energy. It's an energy of prosperity, giving, love, energy of Infinite Goodness. Feel that light reaching you. Feel its power, energy. Feel prosperity in that light. Infinite prosperity from the Universe.

See this golden light relaxing your chest. Breathe in and out this golden light, slowly. Breathe in, in, in, in, in, hold it, hold it, breathe out, out, out, out, out, out out. Breathe in, in, in, in, in, hold it, hold it, breathe out, out, out, out, out, out out. Breathe in, in, in, in, in, hold it, hold it, breathe out, out, out, out, out, out out.

It feels good to breathe light. Feel that you're breathing golden, loving, powerful prosperous light. Feel this light relaxing your chest, melting any tension, any knots. Let this light go down to your stomach, relaxing your organs. Feel how it relaxes you, how it purifies your belly. Let the light relax your hips. Relax.

Feel how this light is cleansing your body, cleansing and making all cells in your body relax in this infinite light.

See this light going to your legs, penetrating its muscles, relaxing all leg muscles, then your feet. Feel this light massaging deeply your feet. Now feel this light coming up your legs to your back. It relaxes and penetrates all your back. It feels good to have this powerful light on your back, relaxing it.

You feel purified and relaxed. Now feel this light and energy on your shoulders. They relax, relax, relax. You feel your shoulders absorbing this golden light and relaxing deeply.

Spread this light to your arms and hands. Feel how your hands are brilliant with this powerful, beautiful, prosperous energy.

Feel this light go up to your shoulders and neck. It relaxes your neck, relaxes it. The light goes to your throat and vocal chords. See your vocal cords vibrating with this gold, prosperous light, feel your throat brilliant with this beautiful, powerful, light. Now let it go to your face. Feel this energy relaxing your face muscles deeply. Feel how your face is now brilliant with this energy. It's an energy of prosperity, it's an energy of love. It's positive energy in every muscle in your face. Feel this energy in your scalp. Feel how it's around your head, relaxing your scalp.

Now feel this energy penetrating your mind, your brain, You feel good. Let this golden light penetrate deeply in every cell in your head.

You're deeply relaxed. Deeply relaxed. You're surrounded and protected in this wonderful golden light.

Imagine you're walking to a beautiful place in nature. See and feel this place. How it smells, feel the wind. Feel that you'rewalking in it.

You're going to find your abundance castle. See it in the distance and walk towards it. Yo"re getting closer and closer to your castle, until you enter it. The door is open for you. and you're going to enter that castle. See what it looks like. What is its floor like? Walls, ceiling. You're going to walk through its rooms. It has tons and tons of beautiful things, and tons of prosperous things, and you can touch them. You see money, maybe some jewels, trip tickets, maybe cars, collectibles, cosmetics. Anything. It has things you like, things you think are prosperous. Touch the things there, the money, jewels, trip tickets, cars, anything. Just go to that place and enjoy the feeling. Continue imagining it, seeing what it's like until you're ready to come back to your physical place and get up. That prosperous energy will be with you.

5

LOVING YOUR ABUNDANCE CASTLE

THIS MEDITATION IS EXPLAINED AND PRACTICED FOR THE FIRST TIME IN DAY 7.

Sit or lie down in a comfortable place. Now think about the Sun, how powerful it is, how much energy and life it sends to Earth. You receive its rays freely. Imagine that you're receiving this gold light of the sun, and that it's literally love from the Universe, prosperous, giving love from the Universe. If you believe in God or any other greater force, imagine that this light carries that energy. It's an energy of prosperity, giving, love, energy of Infinite Goodness. Feel that light reaching you. Feel its power, energy. Feel prosperity in that light. Infinite prosperity from the Universe.

See this golden light relaxing your chest. Breathe in and out this golden light, slowly. Breathe in, in, in, in, in, hold it, hold it, breathe out, out, out, out, out, out out. Breathe in, in, in, in, in, hold it, hold it, breathe out, out, out, out,

out, out out. Breathe in, in, in, in, in, hold it, hold it, breathe out, out, out, out, out, out out.

It feels good to breathe light. Feel that you're breathing golden, loving, powerful prosperous light. Feel this light relaxing your chest, melting any tension, any knots.

Feel that this light is love from the universe. Feel this love. Open up to receive this love.

Now think about a person, a pet, or a memory that gives you feelings of love. Bring up those lovely, lovely feelings.

Feel that warm feeling of love in your chest.

Feel how your chest is so filled with the light of love.

So much love. Love you receive. Love you give. You are loved and you love.

Let this light of love expanding.

Feel now this loving, prosperous light going down to your stomach. You feel a loving feeling in your stomach. Feel it relaxing your hips. All tension is gone from your hips, replaced with pure loving, prosperous energy.

See this light going to your legs, how your legs are imbued with loving, golden prosperous light. Feel this light on your feet and how they are brilliant with this magnificent light. Now feel this light coming up your legs to your back. It feels good to have this powerful light on your back, relaxing it. Feel this powerful energy of universal love and your love on your back. You feel more loving, loved, relaxed.

Now feel this light and energy on your shoulders. They relax, relax, relax. You feel your shoulders absorbing this golden light and relaxing deeply.

Spread this light to your arms and hands. Feel how your hands are brilliant with this powerful, beautiful, prosperous energy. So much love in your hands, ready to give and receive. Your hands are brilliant.

Feel this light go up to your shoulders and neck. It relaxes your neck, relaxes it. The light goes to your throat and vocal chords. See your vocal cords vibrating with this gold, loving, prosperous light, feel your throat brilliant with this beautiful, powerful, light. Now let it go to your face. Feel this energy penetrating and relaxing your face skin and muscles deeply. Feel how your face is now brilliant with this energy. It's an energy of prosperity, it's an energy of love. It's positive energy in every muscle in your face. Feel how your face is incredibly brilliant with this powerful, loving energy. Feel then this energy in your scalp. Feel how it's around your head, relaxing your scalp.

Now feel this energy penetrating your mind, your brain, Your thoughts are imbued with loving, prosperous energy. You feel good. Let this golden light penetrate deeply in every cell in your head.

You're deeply relaxed. Deeply relaxed. You're surrounded

and protected in this wonderful golden light, a golden light carrying your love and the love from the universe.

Bring back that light to your chest. Think again about those loving memories and feel a warmth in your heart. Feel this light expanding, enveloping and protecting you. It feels good to be surrounded in that light.

Imagine you're walking to a beautiful place in nature. See and feel this place. Feel its smells, temperature, feel your feet on the ground, even if you're wearing shoes.

You're going to find your abundance castle. See it in the distance and walk towards it. You're getting closer and closer to your castle, until you enter it. The door is open for you. and you're going to enter that castle.

Before you enter, feel that energy of love, that warm feeling in your chest, and send it as a ray of warm light.

Surround the castle with your love. Now enter it. You can touch things, but also envelop them in this loving, prosperous energy. Everything that you see and like, send it love, envelop it in your energy of prosperity and love. Touch the things there, the money, jewels, trip tickets, cars, anything. Envelop them in love. Enjoy the feeling. Continue imagining appreciating the details in your castle and sending love to them until you're ready to go back to where you are. You'll feel this loving, prosperous energy with you throughout the whole day.

6

CONFRONTING YOUR MONSTER

THIS MEDITATION IS EXPLAINED IN DAY 8.

This meditation is good, but shouldn't be practiced too often. You can do it a couple times in the beginning, but then don't do it more often than once every three months. If you want, you can never do it again.

Sit or lie down in a comfortable place. Now think about the Sun, how powerful it is, how much energy and life it sends to Earth. You receive its rays freely. Imagine that you're receiving this gold light of the Sun, and that it's literally love from the Universe, prosperous, giving love from the Universe. It's an energy of prosperity, giving, love, energy of Infinite Goodness. Feel that light reaching you. Feel its power, energy. Feel prosperity in that light. Infinite prosperity from the Universe.

See this golden light relaxing your chest. Breathe in and out this golden light, slowly. Breathe in, in, in, in, in, hold it, hold it, breathe out, out, out, out, out, out out. Breathe in, in, in, in, in, hold it, hold it, breathe out, out, out, out, out out. Breathe in, in, in, in, in, hold it, hold it, breathe out, out, out, out, out, out out.

It feels good to breathe light. Feel that you're breathing golden, loving, powerful prosperous light. Feel this light relaxing your chest, melting any tension, any knots.

Feel that this light is love from the universe. Feel this love. Open up to receive this love.

Now think about a person, a pet, or a memory that gives you feelings of love. Bring up those lovely, lovely feelings.

Feel that warm feeling of love in your chest.

Feel how your chest is so filled with the light of love.

So much love. Love you receive. Love you give. You are loved and you love.

Let this light of love expanding.

You're surrounded and protected in this wonderful golden light, a golden light carrying your love and the love from the universe. Feel how you're protected. Feel this energy surrounding your entire body, and relax, knowing you're protected. This energy makes you feel so good. You breathe slowly, relax.

Bring back that light to your chest. Think again about those loving memories and feel a warmth in your heart. Feel how those loving feelings feel good. Feel this love, deeply in your heart. Your love. Feel how the universe matches its love with its golden, loving light. Feel these two lights meeting, and how wonderful they make you feel. Feel how this love makes you feel good. It's so good to feel loving. It's so, so good. You relax in those lovely thoughts.

Imagine you're walking to a beautiful place in nature. Feel that the love is still with you. You're a loving and loved person walking in nature. See and feel this place. Smell the air, feel the wind, hear its sounds. It's a lovely place and you're a lovely person.

You're going to find your abundance castle. See it in the distance and walk towards it. But before the castle, there's a monster. A huge monster. It can be a dragon or something else. Imagine that this monster carries your fears, feeling of unworthiness, negative feelings associated with prosperity. This monster doesn't want to let you go in the castle, but you want to go there. You want to enjoy your castle, but there's a monster, a huge monster preventing you.

You feel afraid, but you know how to beat fear. You project love to this monster. Now the monster is no longer threatening. It's calm, even if it's still a monster. Send your love to this monster and walk to it without fear.

Touch or hug a part of it and envelop this monster with love.

As you hug it and envelop it with love, the monster transforms. Slowly, it's becoming a human child. It's you as a child! Hug your inner child, your fearful self. Hug it and envelop your child with powerful, protecting love from the Universe, with your own powerful, protecting love.

It feels good to give love to your vulnerable parts, doesn't it? Now, you're going to go to the castle with your inner child. Explore the place, have fun, enjoy the experience. Your inner child is happy to see the abundance, the prosperity, the money, everything. Your inner child is cured.

Your inner child knows that it's safe to go to your castle of prosperity, knows it's a good, fun, safe place. There's nothing to fear, there's nothing wrong about going in it, there are no negative consequences. You can now hug again your inner child and you two become one. Healed. Imagine you're back in your physical place, surrounded with golden energy.

7

TAKING THE ABUNDANCE CASTLE WITH YOU

THIS MEDITATION IS INTRODUCED AND EXPLAINED IN DAY 9.

S it or lie down in a comfortable place. Now think about the Sun, how powerful it is, how much energy and life it sends to Earth. How it represents prosperity and love from the Universe, freely given. Appreciate these rays, this energy, this abundance. Imagine that you're receiving this gold light of the Sun, and that it's literally love from the Universe, prosperous love from the Universe. It's an energy of prosperity, giving, love, energy of Infinite Goodness. Feel that light reaching you. Feel its power, energy. Feel prosperity in that light. Infinite prosperity from the Universe.

Breathe in and out this golden, loving, prosperous energy, slowly. Breathe in, in, in, in, in, hold it, hold it, breathe out, out, out, out, out, out out. Breathe in, in, in, in, in, hold it, hold it, breathe out, out, out, out, out, out out.

Breathe in, in, in, in, in, hold it, hold it, breathe out, out, out, out, out, out out. It's prosperous, loving, universal energy.

It feels good to breathe light. Feel that you're breathing golden, loving, powerful prosperous light. Feel this light relaxing your chest, melting any tension, any knots.

Feel that this light is love from the universe. Feel this love. Open up to receive this love. Allow this love to reach you.

Now think about a person, a pet, or a memory that gives you feelings of love. Bring up those lovely, lovely feelings.

Feel that warm feeling of love in your chest.

Feel how your chest is so filled with the light of love.

So much love. Love you receive. Love you give. You are loved and you love.

Feel how those loving feelings feel good. Feel this love, deeply in your heart. Your love. Feel how the universe matches its love with its golden, loving light. Feel these two lights meeting, and how wonderful they make you feel. Feel how this love makes you feel good. It's so good to feel loving. It's so, so good. You relax in those lovely thoughts.

You're surrounded and protected in this wonderful, powerful light, a light carrying your love and the love from the universe. Feel how you're protected. Feel this energy surrounding your entire body, and relax, knowing you're protected. This energy makes you feel so good. You breathe slowly, relax. This energy is so, so powerful. Love makes it so powerful.

Imagine now you're walking to a beautiful place in nature, going to your abundance castle. Feel that the love is still with you. You're a loving and loved person walking in nature. See and feel this place. Smell the air, feel the wind, hear its sounds. It's a lovely place and you're a lovely person.

Your inner child is waiting for you, super happy to see you. Hug and envelop your inner child with love. It feels good to give love to your vulnerable parts, doesn't it? Now, you're going to go to the castle with your inner child.

Explore the place, have fun, enjoy the experience. Walk through the castle, notice things you really like. Just walk through the castle. See the money in it. You can see a bathtub filled with cash or coins and jump with it. You and your inner child. Play with the money. It's fun!

You're surrounded in money. Now go to a room where you find things you like, objects you like. It has everything! it's so amazing! You enjoy seeing those things. Your inner child also enjoys it. It's a fun place to be surrounded with abundance, money, prosperity.

Now it's time to go out of the castle. You and your child leave it and look back.

Once you get out, look at the child and say, "Want to take it home?"

The child agrees. The castle transforms itself in golden, sparkly energy. See its walls dissolving and becoming energy, see how the entire castle is slowly transforming in golden, sparkly energy. It's the same castle, with everything in it, but in energy form.

Now see this energy of the castle condensing into a ball of energy. It's the same castle, just in condensed form. Now feel how you're attracting this energy to you. This energy of the castle is attracted to you and your love, your brilliant light. It's attracted, and you don't need to make any effort.

You relax and allow this energy to enter your chest, your heart, then permeate your body. You and the child become one. You are surrounded with that prosperous energy of your abundance castle. You have the castle with you! Now you return to where you were sitting or standing. Feel the energy around you. You have the prosperous energy of the sun, the energy of love, and the energy of the prosperity castle, and you're carrying now the castle with you!

8

CARRYING THE ABUNDANCE CASTLE WITH YOU EVERYWHERE

THIS MEDITATION IS INTRODUCED AND EXPLAINED IN DAY 10

Sit or lie down in a comfortable place. Now think about the Sun, how powerful it is, how much energy and life it sends to Earth. How it represents prosperity and love from the Universe, freely given. Appreciate these rays, this energy, this abundance. Imagine that you're receiving this gold light of the Sun, and that it's love from the Universe, prosperous love from the Universe. It's an energy of prosperity, giving, love, energy of Infinite Goodness. Feel that light reaching you. Feel its power, energy. Feel prosperity in that light. Infinite prosperity from the Universe.

Breathe in and out this golden, loving, prosperous energy, slowly. Breathe in, in, in, in, in, hold it, hold it, breathe out, out, out, out, out, out out. Breathe in, in, in, in, in, hold it, hold it, breathe out, out, out, out, out, out out.

Breathe in, in, in, in, in, hold it, hold it, breathe out, out, out, out, out, out out. It's prosperous, loving, universal energy.

Feel that you're breathing golden, loving, powerful prosperous light. Feel this light relaxing your chest, melting any tension, any knots.

Feel that this light is love from the universe. Feel this love. Open up to receive this love. Allow this love to reach you.

Now think about a person, a pet, or a memory that gives you feelings of love. Bring up those lovely, lovely feelings.

Feel that warm feeling of love in your chest.

Feel how your chest is so filled with the light of love.

So much love. Love you receive. Love you give. You are loved and you love.

Feel how those loving feelings feel good. Feel this love, deeply in your heart. Your love. Feel how the universe matches its love with its golden, loving light. Feel these two lights meeting, and how wonderful they make you feel. Feel how this love makes you feel good. It's so good to feel loving. It's so, so good. You relax in those lovely thoughts.

You're surrounded and protected in this wonderful, powerful light, a light carrying your love and the love from the universe. Feel how you're protected. Feel this energy surrounding your entire body, and relax, knowing you're protected. This energy makes you feel so good. You breathe slowly, relax. This energy is so, so powerful. Love makes it so powerful.

Imagine now you're walking to a beautiful place in nature, going to your abundance castle. Feel that the love is still with you. You're a loving and loved person walking in nature. See and feel this place. Smell the air, feel the wind, hear its sounds. It's a lovely place and you're a lovely person.

You get to the place where your abundance castle usually is, but it's not there. It's normal. See the place where the castle usually is, but without the castle, but feel good about it, knowing that you have the castle with you. Your castle had been transformed in energy, and it's in your chest.

Feel the energy of your abundance castle in your chest. Now see the energy of the castle coming out of your chest, becoming sparkly energy, then forming the walls of the castle again, the way you've always seen it. See it becoming solid, how this energy from your chest forms an abundance castle. It's there, the way it had always been. It's cool to have a portable abundance castle.

Now you can see your inner child coming from you. Your inner child is going there with you, so you have company.

Go in the castle and touch its walls, feel the objects. Enjoy its beauty. Go to the rooms. Go to the bathtub with money or gild and jump in it or just observe it. It's all there. Go to the room with the objects you like. Touch them. Feel how they are solid. Everything is solid and real. The castle has indeed been materialized. Spend time touching the things in the castle. It feels good to know that all of that is there for you.

Feel the textures, feel the smells.

it's real. You're in an abundance castle that feels solid and real, and you are there.

Continue touching it, feeling it. Enjoy the experience of being in this abundance. It feels good. It's a solid abundance castle and you're walking in it.

Enjoy the experience. Look and feel the details.

Walk in it. Touch its things.

It feels good.

Now get ready to go back.

Walk outside the castle, slowly, you and your inner child.

Become one with the child again. You feel strong and loved.

Now transform the castle in sparkly energy and allow it to enter your chest. See its walls becoming golden, sparkly energy, see how it's transforming.

See this energy in a ball of light. It's the same solid castle, but in energy form. It's attracted to you and your beautiful, prosperous loving light. It's yours! Allow it to enter your chest and become one with it. It's your castle and its energy is in you.

Go back to where you are, feel the energy of your castle combined with the energy of the sun, and imagine you are surrounded with that energy. That energy wants to expand, and you allow it to fill the room where you are. Imagine that this energy wants to expand, and you relax and allow it to expand. Feel it permeating the room where you are.

Feel that it goes with you and surrounds you wherever you go. It's prosperous energy, energy you can send to other people when you want, and it will make you feel good.

9
YOU'RE GUIDED BY INFINITE INTELLIGENCE

THIS MEDITATION IS INTRODUCED AND EXPLAINED ON DAY 17. YOU CAN DO IT WHENEVER YOU WANT, ESPECIALLY BEFORE SITUATIONS WHERE YOU'LL NEED TO USE YOUR INTELLIGENCE OR INTUITION.

Lie down or sit comfortably. Feel your breath in and out. Breathe, in, in, in, in, hold it, then out, out, out, out, out. Breathe, in, in, in, in, hold it, then out, out, out, out, out. Feel how you're connected with the world around you, how the universe permeates your body through air. Imagine now the stars in the universe, the billions of stars, and the greatness and wisdom keeping it all together.

Imagine you're breathing this wisdom with the energy of the stars. Breathe in and out slowly, then feel it moving through your body, relaxing, cleaning, inspiring, from your chest, to your tummy, legs, feet, then up to your back, shoulders, arms, hands, back to your shoulder, neck, and throat. Feel this energy cleansing and permetating your throat and vocal chords, imbuing your communication with wisdom. Now feel it in your head. Feel how this energy allows your thoughts to become clearer, allows your mind to vibrate in line with prosperity and wisdom. You're relaxed, quiet.

Now imagine you're going up a set of stairs. You're going to the higher place of knowledge. Feel that you're going up nine steps. One, two, three, four, five, six, seven, eight, nine. Now you arrive at the place of knowledge. Look at that place, what it contains. It has wisdom and knowledge from the universe. It knows past, future. It's infinite, omniscient. All this knowledge is available to you.

Now imagine a higher being from this place of knowledge. This higher being hugs you and tells you they love you. You feel loved, secure, protected. Feel that love from the higher being to you. You are a magnificent child of the universe, unique, with your own path to thread, and your own voice to the world. Feel that hug. Feel how it makes you feel safe, loved, protected. Feel that wonderful feeling of guidance and protection.

Now this higher being is going to take you to a special place in that place of knowledge. It's a transparent chamber with floating sparkles. Those sparkles represent the wisdom of that place of knowledge. Your higher being opens the door to you and you enter this chamber.

You can breathe this sparkly energy. It inspires you. It also permeates and penetrates your body and energetic field.

You feel the wisdom, inspiration, knowledge, intuition from the universe in your life, in your body, in your mind.

You feel that energy cleansing old patterns, resistance, fear. You relax and enjoy your time receiving that wise energy. Feel how you breathe this inspiring, wise energy. Feel it in your body. Feel it around you. Feel how good it is to receive all this omniscient knowledge, to breathe it, to feel this magical inspiration.

Now you go out of the chamber, with that energy in you. You feel deeply inspired. Hug again your higher being. Feel the warmth, love, and protection in that hug. You're deeply loved and guided.

Now you're going back down the stairs. Nine steps. One, two, three, four, fice, six, seven, eight, nine.

Feel yourself back in the physical place where you were. Visualize that energy around you. Feel guided and protected. Feel how it gives you inspiration, confidence, wisdom. Feel how it opens you up for intuition and higher ideas. Feel that energy around you.

Open your eyes. The energy is still with you, and you have the wisdom of the universe to guide you.

10

YOU RECEIVE YOUR LUCKY STAR

THIS MEDITATION IS INTRODUCED AND EXPLAINED ON DAY 22. IT'S A MEDITATION YOU CAN DO WHENEVER YOU WANT.

Sit or lie down in a comfortable place. Now think about the Sun, how powerful it is, how much energy and life it sends to Earth. You receive its rays freely. Imagine that you're receiving this gold light of the Sun, and that it's literally love from the Universe, prosperous, giving love from the Universe. It's an energy of prosperity, giving, love, energy of Infinite Goodness. Feel that light reaching you. Feel its power, its energy. Feel prosperity in that light. Infinite prosperity from the Universe.

See this golden light relaxing your chest. Breathe in and out this golden light, slowly. Breathe in, in, in, in, in, hold it, hold it, breathe out, out, out, out, out, out out. Breathe in, in, in, in, in, hold it, hold it, breathe out, out, out, out, out, out out. Breathe in, in, in, in, in, hold it, hold it, breathe out, out, out, out, out, out out.

It feels good to breathe light. Feel that you're breathing golden, loving, powerful prosperous light. Feel this light relaxing your chest, melting any tension, any knots.

Feel that this light is love from the universe. Feel this love. Open up to receive this love.

Now think about a person, a pet, or a memory that gives you feelings of love. Bring up those lovely, lovely feelings.

Feel that warm feeling of love in your chest.

Feel how your chest is so filled with the light of love.

So much love. Love you receive. Love you give. You are loved and you love.

Let this light of love expanding.

You're surrounded and protected in this wonderful golden light, a golden light carrying your love and the love from the universe. Feel how you're protected. Feel this energy surrounding your entire body, and relax, knowing you're protected. This energy makes you feel so good. You breathe slowly, relax.

Bring back that light to your chest. Think again about those loving memories and feel a warmth in your heart. Feel how those loving feelings feel good. Feel this love, deeply in your heart. Your love. Feel how the universe matches its love with its golden, loving light. Feel these two lights meeting, and how wonderful they make you feel. Feel how this love makes you feel good. It's so good to feel loving. It's so, so good. You relax in those lovely thoughts.

Now you're going to imagine you're going up the stairs to the temple of knowledge.

Imagine you're going up a set of stairs. You're going to the higher place of knowledge. Feel that you'regoing up nine steps. One, two, three, four, five, six, seven, eight, nine. Now you arrive at the place of knowledge. Look at that place, what it contains. It has wisdom and knowledge from the universe. It knows past, future. It's infinite, omniscient. All this knowledge is available to you.

See the place, the details.

Now the higher being is coming to you with a gift. You receive a necklace with a pendant. The pendant is a blue crystal star. You are then told that this is a lucky star, that whenever you wear it you'll be lucky. You're also told that this star is invisible in the material world, so you can wear it whenever you want. Touch this star, it's texture. Feel that you have that pendant on your neck. See how it's a precious gift, feel it's power. Your higher being tells you to go back and carry the star. Hug the higher being. Feel the warmth and love in that hug. Feel protected.

Now you're going back to your physical place.

Go down the stairs. One, two, three, four, five, six, seven, eight, nine.

Fee your body. Feel that you carry the star with you. Luck will be with you from now and always. Remember that you carry that pendant with you.

TAPPING

ABOUT TAPPING

Tapping is introduced and also explained on day 11.

Tapping is also called EFT, or emotional freedom technique. It's a great, fast, and effective way to get rid of anxiety and stored beliefs and negative patterns.

Traditional tapping recognizes and works on negative emotions. It's good to work on negative emotions, but it's a deep cleaning process and must not be done often.

In this book, we'll do slightly different tapping, in the sense that we won't usually focus on negative emotions, so you can do most of these tappings daily.

To do tapping you tap on the side of your hand, then keep tapping on the other points in a circular motion while doing affirmations.

For this book, you can read and tap. If you choose to listen to the audiobook, you might not have time to repeat the affirmations, and in this case you can just tap and think about the words as you hear them and tap along.

The most important is tapping on the points and bringing up the emotions related to the topic you're working on.

The points of tapping are:

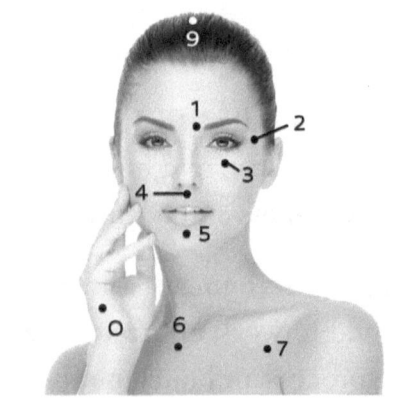

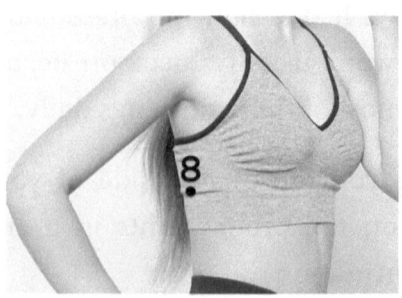

0 - Karate chop. This is the side of your hand between the wrist and your little finger.

1 - Third eye. It's not really your third eye, but the inner part of your eyebrow, near the top of your nose. If you're wearing glasses, you can do it between the eyes.

2 - Temples - outer side of the eye, near where your eyebrow ends.

3 - Under the eye - above the top of your cheekbone, where you would still put concealer to hide circles. Be gentle there.

4 - Under the nose - between your nose and upper lip

5 - Chin - between chin and mouth.

6 - Collarbone - Right where you would have a tie knot

7 - Scapula - It's in the middle of your shoulder blade. If you move your shoulders forward, it's the part that is most depressed in your shoulder blade.

8 - Under your arms. If you wear a bra, it's right over your bra, under your arm. In this place you should tap with the palm of your hands.

9 - Top of your head. Here you can use all of your five fingers.

1

CLEANSING TAPPING FOR NEGATIVE BELIEFS ABOUT MONEY

THIS TAPPING IS INTRODUCED AND EXPLAINED IN DAY 11.

W arning: This is a deep cleansing tapping, and should be done only once, or no more than once every six months, in case you're feeling very negative about money.

This is a cleansing tapping, and it brings up negative emotions. Acknowledging, accepting, forgiving, and moving on from negative emotions is a very important step to overcoming these blocks and limitations, and why this tapping session is so important. It really speeds up your process. That said, do this tapping only once.

Tap on your karate chop point. Repeat: As I am getting

ready to expand and allow more and more prosperity in my life, I choose to let go of old beliefs and habits. Even though I sometimes felt afraid of having money, I forgive and I accept myself deeply and completely. Even though sometimes I felt that I wasn't worthy of having more money, I deeply and completely forgive and accept myself and everyone else who might have contributed to those feelings. Even though sometimes I felt that life was unfair to me, or that somehow I had bad luck or wasn't destined for prosperity, I choose to love and accept myself, and, most of all, forgive myself, for this and any other limiting beliefs I held in the past. Even though sometimes I decided to aim low, for fear of disappointment, I choose to deeply and completely love, forgive, and accept myself. I deeply and completely accept myself despite any limiting or misguided beliefs or feelings I have held in the past. I'm now healing and moving on.

Tap on your third eye. Sometimes in the past, I might have felt that I didn't deserve money, or that I shouldn't ask for more money.

Tap on the side of your eye. I felt that I wasn't good enough, or that life came with a limit, a limit I shouldn't dare pass.

Tap under your eye. Maybe I was afraid, maybe I thought that having more money was wrong, maybe I decided to settle for less so as not to be disappointed.

Tap under the nose: Maybe I just didn't know better.

Tap on your chin. Some of these feelings might have caused me to feel bad. I even might have felt jealous, angry, upset, disappointed, shameful.

Tap on your collarbone. These feelings were not fun and were not nice, and the reason they made me feel bad was because they were not in alignment with my true self.

Tap on your scapula. My true self is prosperous and believes in infinite source and abundance. My true self knows that it deserves anything it wants, and I'm ready to embrace my true feelings of prosperity.

Tap under your arm. I choose to release any and every negative feeling and limiting beliefs about money from my body, mind, and energetic field now and forever.

Tap on the top of your head. I release any feelings of envy or discomfort about other people when they have prosperity. I understand that there's enough prosperity to go around, and I understand that I can have as much as other people, and each of us is unique.

Tap on your third eye. I release any feelings that I should ask for little or limit myself to little. There's no need for me to limit myself. I allow myself to reach for the stars. If anything, it feels much, much better!

Tap on the side of your eye. I release any feeling that I'm not worthy. I'm a wonderful, unique, magnificent child of the universe, and I deserve good things. My worthy is infinite. I am worthy.

Tap under your eye. I let go of the need to limit myself. There's beauty in struggle, but there's also beauty in achievement, there's beauty in reaching for more, achieving my dreams, helping people.

Tap under your nose. I let go of any fear that money might be dangerous for me or for the people around me. I feel the good that I can do with money, and I decide to allow more and more money in my life.

Tap on your chin. I choose to align myself with prosperity, and to allow prosperity and money in my life, mind, body, and energetic field.

Tap on your collarbone. I feel the energy of money and abundance entering my life, and I allow more and more of it.

Tap on your scapula. I choose to release from my body, my mind, my spirit, and my energetic field any fear, any limiting belief, any negative thought that has kept money away from me in the past. It feels good and natural to let go of these old beliefs. My real nature is prosperous.

Tap under your arm. I feel great now that I have got rid of any feelings that don't serve my prosperous nature. I feel great now that I'm open to my true prosperity, now that I recognize my real worth.

Tap on the top of your head. I choose to allow more and more money in my life, and I know it's safe, it's good, and it's in line with my inner self.

Tap on your third eye. I can do good with money, I deserve as much money as I want, and I choose to align myself with abundance and prosperity.

Tap beside your eye. I vibrate in alignment with prosperity. I attract money and opportunities, and I manifest my true self and my ideal life. I feel great about it.

Tap under your eye. I love money and money loves me. I love to see prosperity in my life and in other people's lives.

Tap on your chin. I understand that I'm worthy of money, and this understanding fills me with happiness and warmth.

Tap on your collarbone. I feel thankful for all the money that I have and all the money that's on my way. I know I deserve it, and I'm excited to use it.

Tap on your scapula. Money brings me joy, and this joyous feeling attracts more and more money in my life. I'm excited, thankful, and happy.

Tap under your arm. It feels great to allow money, and I feel great right now.

Tap on the top of your head. It feels great to let abundance and prosperity permeate my thoughts, my body, and my energetic field. I embrace it in my life.

Now take a deep breath. How do you feel?

2

FEELING GOOD ABOUT MONEY

THIS TAPPING IS INTRODUCED AND EXPLAINED IN DAY 12.
YOU CAN DO THIS TAPPING SESSION AS OFTEN AS
YOU WANT.

Take a deep breath, and think about your relationship with money.

Tap on your karate chop: I'm ready to open up for more prosperity, abundance, money. I allow prosperity in my life, and allow more and more prosperous thoughts. I choose to believe that money is good, that I deserve it, and that I am worthy of everything I want. I choose to aim for prosperity and abundance, with the deep knowledge that I deserve it. I release any feelings of fear, unworthiness or doubt while at the same time forgiving and loving myself deeply and completely.

Tap on your third eye: I allow abundance in my life. I release any fear, limitation, or misguided thoughts that could interfere with this abundance.

Tap on the side of your eye: I choose to feel good about money, and feel confident in my ability to attract money and to keep money.

Tap under your eye: I feel prosperity increasing in my life. I allow it to increase, I feel it increasing, and I feel great about it.

Tap under your nose: More and more prosperous thoughts come to me. I feel aligned with prosperity, aligned with money, and attracting money.

Tap on your chin: It feels good to allow money to come to me. It feels good to increase my prosperity.

Tap on your collarbone: It feels natural to let money come to me, and to attract opportunities.

Tap on your scapula: Feeling good about money feels right, feels natural.

Tap under your arm: More and more I see my prosperity increasing, and I feel good about it.

Tap on the top of your head: it's natural to have extra money in my bank account, and I love having extra money there.

Tap on your third eye: it's great to always have extra money, and to have more and more extra money every month.

Tap on the side of your eye: I feel that I'm expanding my ability to attract money, and money is coming to me more easily.

Tap under your eye: More and more I'm getting better paid for what I do or what I sell. I get better clients, better opportunities, bringing me more and more money.

Tap under your nose: I allow good opportunities to come to me because I know I'm worthy and deserving of them.

Tap on your chin: I'm confident in my ability to attract money, and to be valued and appreciated for the wonderful being that I am.

Tap on your collarbone: I feel that I'm worthy, deserving, valuable, and it's natural that the universe recognizes that and brings me prosperity.

Tap on your scapula: I am confident and happy about having more and more money in my life. I deserve it and I can do a lot of good with money. I enjoy feeling the energy of prosperity in my body, mind, and energetic field.

Tap under your arm: I'm excited about having more money. It fills me with joy and happy anticipation. I enjoy vibrating in harmony with prosperity.

Tap on the top of your head: I expect good things to happen, I expect money to come to me.

Tap on your third eye: it's natural for me to attract great, well paid opportunities.

Tap on the side of your eye: I see my bank account with more and more extra money every month, and it's natural.

Tap under your eye: I see better and better, greatly well paid opportunities coming my way. I know they are right for me and I deserve them.

Tap under your nose: It feels right to earn a lot of money, it feels natural. I feel great about it, calm and confident.

Tap on your chin: I enjoy having a lot of money, and I enjoy spending it and spreading prosperity around me.

Tap on your collarbone: it's right for me to earn a lot of money.

Tap on your scapula: It feels natural to see my bank account with more and more extra money every month.

Tap under your arm: It feels good to know deeply that I'm worthy and deserving of great prosperity.

Tap on the top of your head. I'm happy to be aligned with the energy of money. I allow this energy in my body, mind, and energetic field.

3

ALLOWING INFINITE INTELLIGENCE TO GUIDE YOU

THIS TAPPING SESSION IS INTRODUCED ON DAY 16. YOU CAN DO IT WHENEVER YOU WANT AND IT'S HELPFUL ESPECIALLY BEFORE MAKING DECISIONS OR DOING ANYTHING WHERE INTELLIGENCE AND WISDOM WILL BE HELPFUL.

Take a deep breath, and imagine yourself being guided and protected.

Tap on your karate chop: Today I recognize that there's an infinite intelligence that knows more than I do. I choose to trust this higher power and infinite intelligence. I choose to allow it to guide and inspire me. I deeply and completely appreciate the fullness of who I am and I choose to relax and allow infinite intelligence to guide me.

Tap on your third eye: I open up for infinite intelligence. I feel myself relaxing and opening up for this powerful energy.

Tap on the side of your eye: I choose to relax and surrender, and realize that I can count on higher inspiration.

Tap under your eye: It feels good not to need to control or decide everything, and instead to feel deeply inspired.

Tap under your nose: I relax. Surrender. Trust the universe to guide me, to give me better ideas, to point me in prosperous directions.

Tap on your chin: I release any fear or resistance to trusting the higher intelligence.

Tap on your collarbone: I attune my intuition to prosperity, and allow it to guide me into a more abundant, fulfilled life.

Tap on your scapula: I know that I'm still in control of my fate, I'm just having help to achieve what I really want, I'm accepting powerful help to fulfill my plein potential.

Tap under your arm: I surrender to a higher intelligence, a higher power, and I open up to its guidance and inspiration.

Tap on the top of your head: I choose to act in alignment with prosperity, and to trust the universe to guide me into this alignment.

Tap on your third eye: It feels good to be attuned to my intuition, it feels good to open up to infinite intelligence and infinite wisdom.

Tap on the side of your eye: I release any need to block or judge this guidance from infinite intelligence, and I allow it to direct me to prosperity and fulfillment.

Tap under your eye: More and more I recognize signs of infinite intelligence guiding me, and it feels great.

Tap under your nose: I feel sudden bursts of inspiration. Amazing ideas come to my mind. I allow these ideas to flow and materialize.

Tap on your chin: My goals become clearer, better, in line with my inner self, in line with prosperity.

Tap on your collarbone: My ideas are sharper, smarter, they lead me to prosperity and fulfillment faster and more easily.

Tap on your scapula: I allow myself to be guided and compelled into deeply inspired action. I feel magnificent, infinite inspiration, and I know how to act on it.

Tap under your arm: I allow infinite intelligence to guide my choices. My choices are smarter, more and more prosperous every day.

Tap on the top of your head. My decisions, inspired by infinite intelligence, are lucky, they take me to prosperous places, they take me to prosperity. I often find myself at the right place and right time.

Tap on your third eye: I allow and trust infinite intelligence to guide me into reaching for goals that are right for me, that bring me the prosperity I want, the fulfillment I want.

Tap on the side of your eye: I relax and trust the universe to inspire me, to guide me, to direct me.

Tap under your eye: I feel active and inspired, and act on ideas from infinite intelligence.

Tap under your nose: I feel like more and more my life is guided into more prosperity, I'm being compelled into prosperous directions.

Tap on your chin: It feels great to be so magnificently inspired, to feel so magnificently encouraged, receive so many magnificent ideas.

Tap on your collarbone: I accept and act on infinite, omniscient intelligence and inspiration, and it feels great to count on such a powerful ally.

Tap on your scapula: Everyday I feel more and more inspired, with clearer goals, making better and better choices, attracting infinite prosperity into my life, tapping into infinite wisdom.

Tap under your arm: I choose to work in line with infinite wisdom, and I trust this powerful guidance. I fine tune my intuition and let it guide me into prosperity.

Tap on the top of your head. My mind opens to amazing ideas, amazing inspiration and it feels great to be connected with this infinite intelligence.

Now take a deep breath. Feel how you're guided and protected. Be open for bursts of inspiration, clearer ideas, and intuition.

4

EXPANDING YOUR BELIEF IN PROSPERITY

THIS TAPPING IS EXPLAINED ON DAY 18, AND YOU CAN DO IT AS OFTEN AS YOU LIKE. IT'S ABOUT EXPANDING YOUR IDEA OF PROSPERITY.

Tap on your karate chop: Today I choose to expand my idea of prosperity, expand my belief of what I can do, achieve, or have. I choose to release any feelings or beliefs in limitations, that I'm not good enough, that I'm unworthy, or that I should settle for less. I choose to release those thoughts, beliefs and feelings from my life, mind, body, and energetic field, from now and forever. Still, I deeply and completely forgive, love, appreciate, and accept myself. I appreciate the fullness of who I am, where my journey has brought me, and where it's leading me. I learn from the past, appreciate what I've learned, and I'm ready to move on with a new outlook in life and new, better-serving beliefs about myself and what I can achieve.

Tap on your third eye: I choose to expand my beliefs

about the prosperity I can achieve. I feel my idea of prosperity expanding, and it feels good.

Tap on the side of your eye: I choose to let go of any limiting beliefs, thoughts, feelings about prosperity. I release them from my body, mind, spirit, and energetic field now and forever.

Tap under your eye: I choose to believe in an infinite universe, and believe that I can connect with the fullness of its power and wisdom.

Tap under your nose: I increase, in my mind, the income I can have. I let it increase, increase, increase. I see it increasing in my bank statement, and it feels good.

Tap on your chin: It feels good to feel this increase, expansion, increase in prosperity, expansion in abundance, this feeling of plenty.

Tap on your collarbone: I know deeply and completely that I am worthy and deserving, and I am worthy of this expansion of prosperity.

Tap on your scapula: I allow my mind to encompass more, believe I deserve and can achieve more, believe in my infinite worth, believe in my connection to the infinite power of the universe.

Tap under your arm: I release any blocks, fears or limitations about the prosperity I can achieve and allow my natural prosperity to flow through me.

Tap on the top of your head: Prosperity allows me to share prosperity, increase prosperity around me, and spread love. I enjoy spreading more and more prosperity around me.

Tap on your third eye: I embrace the prosperity and abundance of the universe. It's infinite, limitless, powerful. It feels good to embrace it.

Tap on the side of your eye: I allow more and more abundance, more and more prosperity, more and more money into my life and the lives of people around me.

Tap under your eye: I am worthy and deserving, and I can see my income growing and growing. It feels good, it feels natural to allow it to grow. I see higher and higher amounts on my bank statement.

Tap under your nose: The more I earn, the more I can spread prosperity around me, the more good I can do I feel happy and thankful to do more and more good.

Tap on your chin: I'm worthy and deserving of high amounts of money, and I open myself for higher and higher amounts. I see higher and higher amounts in my life.

Tap on your collarbone: I'm worthy and deserving of amazing prosperity. I'm the one who decides its limits, and I choose to expand those limits.

Tap on your scapula: More and more I see myself as rich, prosperous, successful, achieving. More and More I see that it's my true nature. I see this prosperity increasing, I feel that I can be more and more successful.

Tap under your arm: Any blocks, fears, limitations, or negative feelings are released from my life, my experience, and my energetic field now and forever.

Tap on the top of your head: It feels good to allow more and more. It feels good to expand. It feels good to see my prosperity increase and increase and increase.

Take a deep breath.

Feel how your feeling of prosperity, your beliefs of how much you can earn have expanded.

5
LOVING AND ATTRACTING SUCCESS

THIS TAPPING IS INTRODUCED AND EXPLAINED ON DAY 21. THIS IS AN EXCELLENT EXERCISE TO DO BEFORE A JOB INTERVIEW OR ANY ACTIVITY WHERE YOU WANT TO FEEL COMPETENT AND SUCCESSFUL.

Tap on your karate chop: Today I'm opening myself to success, to feelings of success, to a true belief that I can be successful in all my endeavors. I deeply and completely appreciate, love, and forgive the fullness of who I am and the path that brought me to this moment. I'm ready for new, more and more successful flight, and it feels great to be ready.

Tap on your third eye: I open up for success. I open up for success to enter my life.

Tap on the side of your eye: I allow success in my life. I know I deserve success, I'm worthy of success.

Tap under your eye: I connect to the higher intelligence of the universe, and it allows me to have success and spread this wisdom and love to the world.

Tap under your nose: I feel the energy of success more and more present in my life, my thoughts. I'm inspired towards success, I act towards success.

Tap on your chin: It feels good to recognize that I can be successful, that I can let the magnificence of my being shine a light in the world.

Tap on your collarbone: It feels great to allow success, to flow with the energy of success, and let it guide me.

Tap on your scapula: Success is something that is good for the people around me and good to the world. My success spreads joy and love.

Tap under your arm: It feels great to feel deeply that I am worthy of great success. I feel excited and eager to spread love to the world.

Tap on the top of your head: Opening up and allowing success feels natural to me. It feels good to allow more and more success.

Tap on your third eye: I allow the energy of success to permeate my thoughts, my actions, my vibration, and it feels so good, I allow it more and more.

Tap on the side of your eye: I feel the energy of success in my energetic field. It goes with me wherever I go, a bright beacon of love. It feels so good!

Tap under your eye: I allow my heart to open up and expand, and transform unconditional, universal love in success, spreading love to the world. So much love!

Tap under your nose: I feel successful, I think successful thoughts, I make successful actions, I aim for successful goals.

Tap on your chin: I am connected to the wisdom of the universe, and I am confident that I have all it takes to achieve great heights.

Tap on your collarbone: I let go of any need to block, resist, or fear my natural path to success. Any resistance has been eliminated from my body, mind, and energetic field now and forever.

Tap on your scapula: I'm so thankful for having the chance to spread love to the world, to achieve my full potential, to reach success in my endeavors.

Tap under your arm: My natural path is aimed towards success, and it feels good to be in line with my magnificent, true nature.

Tap on the top of your head: I allow myself to shine. My light is good for the world.

Now take a deep breath.

You should feel a lot more confident and successful!

6

LOVING AND ATTRACTING LUCK

THIS TAPPING IS INTRODUCED AND EXPLAINED ON DAY 23. THERE'S ALSO SOME EXPLANATION ABOUT LUCK ON DAY 22. THIS IS A FUN TAPPING AND YOU CAN DO IT AS MUCH AS YOU WANT.

Tap on your karate chop: Today I choose to open myself for luck. Pure luck. Why not? Luck is only a manifestation of my energy, my alignment. I choose to be aligned with prosperity, and therefore I attract luck and I deserve it.

Tap on your third eye: I open myself for luck. Luck is good, luck is fun, and I open up for it.

Tap on the side of your eye: I align with prosperity and abundance, and this alignment brings me a lot of luck.

Tap under your eye: I'm worthy and deserving of being lucky. I can worthy of seeing things working out by themselves, and sometimes achieving things without any effort.

Tap under your nose: it's fine to achieve things, win things, or gain things by pure luck, and I choose to allow luck to help me.

Tap on your chin: I feel great to be lucky. I feel appreciation for so much luck in my life, for how things just magically work out.

Tap on your collarbone: My magical blue lucky star is with me at all times, and it's attracting luck wherever I go, and especially when I remember that I'm super lucky.

Tap on your scapula: It feels so great to allow luck in my life, to see that things flow more smoothly, that things work out well, and sometimes better than expected.

Tap under your arm: Luck is now part of my life. Luck permeates my body, mind, and energetic field. It feels good to be lucky and allow so much luck in my life.

Tap on the top of your head: Luck is fun, luck is good, luck is something that I appreciate. I feel good to be lucky.

Tap on your third eye: I love luck everywhere. I love seeing the universe doing its magic just because. I love being in line with this energy.

Tap on the side of your eye: I love seeing people get lucky. It's great for them and I'm happy for them. It feels good to see luck.

Tap under your eye: Getting lucky is a valid way to reach my goals. I allow it because I deserve it.

Tap under your nose: Luck is the name people give to fast manifestation they don't understand. I like fast manifestation therefore I like luck.

Tap on your chin: Being lucky is fun and I enjoy it. It feels great to see the universe in action, making things easy for me, and even bringing me surprises.

Tap on your collarbone: My lucky star is always with me, bringing me luck, making things work out easily, helping me when things seem random.

Tap on your scapula: It feels good to allow luck, to allow the universe to work its magic in my life. I feel luck all around me, I feel lucky energy, and I see lucky results.

Tap under your arm: Luck permeates my body, mind, and energetic field. I'm surrounded by luck, I project luck, I expect luck, and I get luck.

Tap on the top of your head: It feels good to allow luck in my life, and allow its magic to bring me prosperity easily.

7
FOCUSING ON YOUR MAIN GOAL

THIS TAPPING IS EXPLAINED AND INTRODUCED ON DAY 26.
THIS IS A GREAT TAPPING TO MAKE SURE YOU'RE FOCUSED
AND MOVING TOWARDS YOUR GOALS.

To start, visualize your goal. Imagine your goal being achieved. Imagine it until you feel it's a reality. See and feel the details of it. Now let's start tapping.

Tap on your karate chop: I have a goal, and it's a great goal, because I am choosing something that aligns with my true self. I choose to focus on my goat and take inspired action towards it. I choose to move towards plenty fulfillment, and prosperity, and I'm doing it without distraction.

Tap on your third eye: I choose to focus on my true goals, real goals, goals that are good for me, that align with who I am.

Tap on the side of your eye: My effor, energy and

thoughts are directed towards things that matter, that will make my life more fulfilling and prosperous.

Tap under your eye: I no longer choose or get distracted with crappy goals. Instead, I'm focused and determined to achieve what I really want.

Tap under your nose: I am deeply inspired and guided by infinite intelligence, and I allow this intelligence to act through me.

Tap on your chin: I'm compelled into inspired action, and it feels good to let this inspiration flow through me.

Tap on your collarbone: I am on the path of achieving my goals, and it's natural to be on this path, my true self's path. I feel good in it.

Tap on your scapula: It feels great to allow greater inspiration to direct me towards my goal, to guide me and incite inspired action.

Tap under your arm: I am focused, excited, inspired, and I let go of any resistance or fear about my goal.

Tap on the top of your head: I am worthy and deserving of achieving my true goals, and I know I am capable of achieving them.

Tap on your third eye: I'm aligned with success, and I'll bring success to whatever I set out to do.

Tap on the side of your eye: I'm aligned with luck, and I'll bring this great luck to my goals.

Tap under your eye: I step forward with confidence and grace, knowing that the universe is backing me up and I am ready to reach greater heights.

Tap under your nose: With the wisdom and luck of the universe on my side, I'm unstoppable and I'm using this unstoppable energy towards goals that matter.

Tap on your chin: I love taking deeply inspired action, and seeing my goals getting closer and closer. It feels good to know I can achieve my goals.

Tap on your collarbone: My lucky star is here to help me, and I know it will help me on my way.

Tap on your scapula: it's amazing to know that I have everything I need to achieve what I want and that I'm going in that direction.

Tap under your arm: My body, mind, spirit, and energetic field are aligned with my true goals, and the universe is aligning for it.

Tap on the top of your head: I choose to focus on my goals and bring huge prosperity for my life.

Take a deep breath.

VISUALIZATIONS

ABOUT VISUALIZATIONS
THEY ARE INTRODUCED AND FIRST EXPLAINED ON DAY 15.

Visualizations are different from guided meditations. The idea is not to go on a trippy journey, but rather to visualize something that becomes real in your life. It's excellent for setting goals, intentions, etc.

Since you're awake and aware, you must do them sitting, but it's a good idea to slow down your breath and calm down.

it's also a good idea to have your palms facing up. This is not silly. Sit and take a deep breath with your palms down. See how you feel. Now do it with your palms facing up. See the difference?

Visualizations are faster than guided meditations. A trick to make them work is to feel, really feel whatever you are visualizing, make it real.

1

ALLOW A HIGHER POWER TO INSPIRE YOU

THIS VISUALIZATION IS INTRODUCED AND EXPLAINED ON DAY 15.

Sit down with your spine straight, palms facing up and feel comfortable.

Close your eyes. Now breathe in, in, in, in, in, hold it, hold it, now out, out, out, out, out, out, out. Breathe in, in, in, in, in, hold it, hold it, now out, out, out, out, out, out, out. Breathe in, in, in, in, in, hold it, hold it, now out, out, out, out, out, out, out. Breathe in, in, in, in, in, hold it, hold it, now out, out, out, out, out, out, out.

Imagine a silver and purple light coming from above. It's the light of the higher intelligence. Higher intuition. Feel it entering your mind and your energetic field. Imagine that this is a light containing higher intelligence; intelligence from the universe, your subconscious, the collective conscious, a superior power or god, your higher self, or all of it. Allow this light to reach you. Open up and let this light reach you.

See this light reaching you and how you're allowing it.

Say or think these words:

Today I choose to allow infinite intelligence to guide me.

I open up and allow it.

I open up to infinite guidance so that I can set my true goals with clarity.

I allow infinite intelligence to help me set more prosperous goals, in line with my true self.

It feels good to allow infinite intelligence to guide me.

Imagine now this light of infinite intelligence, infinite wisdom. Imagine you're receiving it, you're opening up and receiving it. Feel happy and thankful for receiving this guidance. Feel inspired. Feel trust in your higher guidance. Feel safe. See this light inspiring you. Feel that you are truly receiving this light of higher inspiration.

Take deep breaths. Breath in and out. You're still receiving this light. Open your eyes. See this energy around you. Feel that this light is going to guide you from now on, and be open to sudden bursts of inspiration or intuition.

Try to feel throughout your day that you're being inspired by a higher intelligence.

2

SEE YOUR MAIN GOAL ACHIEVED

THIS VISUALIZATION IS INTRODUCED IN DAY 19. YOU CAN DO IT ONCE A WEEK.

Sit down with your spine straight, and put your hands with palms facing up. Take a slow, deep breath. Breathe in, in, in, in, in, hold it, then out, out, out, out, out, out, out. Breathe in, in, in, in, in, hold it, then out, out, out, out, out, out, out. Breathe in, in, in, in, in, hold it, then out, out, out, out, out, out, out. Keep breathing slowly, notice how you feel more relaxed, calm, how your thoughts get clearer. Now close your eyes. Feel a loving energy on your chest. Feel a prosperous light around you. Feel that you're guided and protected.

it's now two years from now, and you're doing what you decided you want to do, and with the income you want.

See yourself performing your duties or taking care of your company. Focus on your feeling of accomplishment, success. Feel how you feel competent and appreciated.

Feel how you enjoy your work. Feel some physical details. Smell something. Touch something. It's a reality. You're doing it. It's real. Feel competent, satisfied.

Now let's take a look at your bank account or other place where you can see your income, like an income statement. See yourself looking at it. Feel happy for that amount of money. See yourself looking at it, appreciating it. See the income or amount you've made for yourself.

See the kind of clothes you're wearing, the kind of place you live, and more details about your life. See it. Feel it.

it's a reality.

Now say, "This reality, or even better, is in my life now."

Open your eyes. It's a reality in your energy, in the blueprint of your life.

it's already planted, on its way to manifesting. Energetically, it's already a reality in your life. After this visualization, relax and don't focus too much on it.

3

IMBUE YOUR WORK WITH LOVE TO ATTRACT SUCCESS

THIS VISUALIZATION IS INTRODUCED AND EXPLAINED ON DAY 20.

Sit comfortably, but with your spine straight, and have your hands with palms up.

Breathe in slowly, very slowly, very slowly then out slowly, slowly, slowly, slowly, slowly. Breathe in slowly, very slowly, very slowly then out slowly, slowly, slowly, slowly, slowly.Breathe in slowly, very slowly, very slowly then out slowly, slowly, slowly, slowly, slowly.

You feel centered, calm, serene. Imagine a person, a pet, or a memory that evokes feelings of love on your chest. Feel the warmth of this love in your heart. Feel this love. Connect with this feeling of love. So much love. Feel the warmth in your chest. Feel this powerful love.

Feel that it's a light, and that in the invisible world, it's like a beacon. Imagine you can see this light shining from far away, that it's a beacon of love.

Now you're going to imbue your work, your activity, something you create, with that energy of love.

Feel that your work is now brilliant with love, it's also like a beacon. See your work brilliant and energized, magnetic with love.

Now feel this energy of love expanding and reaching out to potential clients or audience. Feel that it's touching the hearts of a lot of people, depending on the potential reach of your activity. Feel that people are being attracted to your work. Feel that people are feeling better, are feeling positive feelings when in the presence of your work. Feel how your love, through your work, benefits a lot of people.

Feel that potential clients or audience feel attracted to your work. Feel that the love in it makes it magnetic. People who can benefit from your work feel attracted to it, they are directed towards your work, they'll come to your work. Feel how your work is attracting people. Now feel how it's spreading love to the world.

Now feel this feeling of love in your chest. Feel the good feeling of sending love to other people. It feels good to give. You feel accomplished, happy, successful. You're happy to spread love. You're happy to help the world increase its vibrations. Feel the immensity and power of the love flowing through you to your work and to other people. Feel how it warms your heart, how it makes you feel good.

Now open your eyes. Feel that love with you.

4

SEE YOUR GOAL FOR ONE MONTH FROM NOW

THIS VISUALIZATION IS INTRODUCED AND EXPLAINED ON DAY 24.

Remember that it's important to visualize something you think you can achieve. Have enough details that it feels real, but leave things open for the universe to work its magic.

Sit down with your spine straight and hands with the palms up, and close your eyes. Take a slow, deep breath. Breathe in, in, in, in, hold it, hold it, then out, out, out, out, out, out. Breathe in, in, in, in, hold it, hold it, then out, out, out, out, out, out. Keep breathing slowly.

Feel that you're connected with a golden energy of prosperity from the universe. Just quiet your mind and feel this connection.

Now see yourself in one month. See your bank account,

or anything tangible where you can see your prosperity. Feel satisfied, calm, happy about it. Imagine how you feel about it. See yourself in the scene. Feel how it's a reality. Feel the textures, the smells. See yourself in it. See yourself with your prosperity goal for one month. It's real. See how it's solid, read. See yourself in it. Feel the details. Feel truly and deeply what you feel with that goal achieved. It's real. Now say: This or better is a reality in my life.

Take a deep breath and let it go. It's sent to the universe.

MORE EXERCISES

MORE EXERCISES

Here's a compilation of some exercises found in this book, in case you want to find them quickly.

1. Send love to prosperity

This is meant to align you with prosperity. You know when you see someone with the job you'd like to have, or the car you'd like, the house and so on? Send it love. Send love to the house, car, or activity. You can even send love to the person. Bring up feelings of love in your chest and send it to this prosperity, as in a colored ray of energy.

2. Send love to prosperity, luck, and success

This is the same as the previous exercise. Did you see

someone who got something by pure luck? Well, luck is good. Send it love. It means you won't have negative feelings and won't impact your own ability to attract luck. You can also send love to success, and it doesn't matter why someone is successful.

3. Surround yourself with prosperous energy and send it to people and places

If you do the meditation about the golden light, you'll do this more easily. Imagine a golden energy of prosperity and surround yourself in it. Now send it to someone or to a place. You can send it to someone when you conduct business with them, for example, or send it to your place of work.

4. Send love to your work and see this love connecting with its audience.

Feel love in your chest and imbue your work, activity, or business with love. See this love reaching people's hearts, making them feel good about your work, and attracting them.

. . .

5. Set the intention to receive guidance from Infinite Intelligence before sleeping

it's what the title says. Before sleeping, ask for guidance. It's likely that your own subconscious will work on finding answers, and who knows what other sources of guidance will help you? You can also use this when you need to pick a goal. We used it a lot in this book.

6. Stop and ask: Where do I want to go? Where is this leading me?

Think about your actions and your choices. Are they helping you be who you are? Are they in line with who you are? Stop and think. It makes a world of difference.

A FINAL WORD

Keep it up. Keep your goals in mind. Work towards them. And don't forget to take some time every week to work on your mind and your ideas of prosperity.

Everything starts in the mind, starts as desire, intention, energy. Keep working on it. Don't forget to put it in action, because energy doesn't like to stagnate.

You're a wonderful being of the universe, and it's been a pleasure to spend 28 days with you.

Sign up for my mailing list at yourmind.fun if you want to hear about new releases and get access to freebies and prizes.

Elwyn Haynes.

www.ingramcontent.com/pod-product-compliance
Lightning Source LLC
Chambersburg PA
CBHW020520080526
44583CB00013B/668